Raised Bed Gardening for Beginners

The Essential Guide to Start and Sustain a Thriving Garden and to Grow Organic Vegetables, Herbs and Fruit.

by

Kevin S. Stevenson

Kevin S. Stevenson
RAISED BED GARDENING FOR BEGINNERS

© Copyright 2022 by Kevin S. Stevenson - **All rights reserved**.

This Book is provided with the sole purpose of providing relevant information on a specific topic for which every reasonable effort has been made to ensure that it is both accurate and reasonable. Nevertheless, by purchasing this Book, you consent to the fact that the author, as well as the publisher, are in no way experts on the topics contained herein, regardless of any claims as such that may be made within. As such, any suggestions or recommendations that are made within are done so purely for entertainment value. It is recommended that you always consult a professional prior to undertaking any of the advice or techniques discussed within.

This is a legally binding declaration that is considered both valid and fair by both the Committee of Publishers Association and the American Bar Association and should be considered as legally binding within the United States.

The reproduction, transmission, and duplication of any of the content found herein, including any specific or extended information, will be done as an illegal act regardless of the end form the information ultimately takes. This includes copied versions of the work, both physical, digital, and audio, unless express consent of the Publisher is provided beforehand. Any additional rights reserved.

Furthermore, the information that can be found within the pages described forthwith shall be considered both accurate and truthful when it comes to the recounting of facts. As such, any use, correct or incorrect, of the provided information will render the Publisher free of responsibility as to the actions taken outside of their direct purview. Regardless, there are zero scenarios where the original author or the Publisher can be deemed liable in any fashion for any damages or hardships that may result from any of the information discussed herein.

Additionally, the information in the following pages is intended only for informational purposes and should thus be thought of as universal. As befitting its nature, it is presented without assurance regarding its prolonged validity or interim quality. Trademarks that are mentioned are done without written consent and can in no way be considered an endorsement from the trademark holder.

Kevin S. Stevenson
RAISED BED GARDENING FOR BEGINNERS

Contents

CHAPTER 1 - Garden with Raised Bed 7
    What is the bed for? 8
    Materials for more depth 9
    How is the bottom of your garden beds? 11
    Custom blends 12
    Annual supply of the raised bed 14

CHAPTER 2 - How to Grow on Raised Beds 17

CHAPTER 3 - How to Build a Raised Bed, Step by Step 21
    Materials needed and Procedure 22
    Create a vegetable garden inside pots and vases 24

CHAPTER 4 – Raised garden in 6 easy steps 27

CHAPTER 5 – 10 Ideas for Making a Functional and Aesthetic Raised Bed 31
    Structures for a Raised Garden 31
        Wooden chests 34
        Masonry raised garden 35
        Gabions to fill with stones 36
        Pallet 38
        Old Furniture 39
        Earthenware Pots 39
        Aluminium bathtub 40
        Pneumatic Tires 41
        Cement blocks 41
        Special shape 42
    The advantages of a raised garden 42
    The disadvantages of the Raised Garden 44

CHAPTER 6 - What's the Point of Planting? 45
    What to plant in the garden: the calendar month by month 48

CHAPTER 7 – Plant Profiles 53
    Vertical Strawberry Growing 53

- Growing in big baskets 54
- Growing in old gutters 55
- Vertical growing in PVC pipes 56
- Strawberries grown in pots 57

Arugula 58

Asparagus 61

Aubergine 69

Basil 75

Beans 82

Broccoli 84

Carrots 87

Celery 94

Cucumber 97

Fennel 106

Lettuce 110

Melon 115

Mint 120

Onion 121

Oregano in pots 130

Parsnip 132

Peas in pots 138

Peppers 142

Potatoes 147

Pumpkin 154

Radishes 159

Rhubarb 162

Spinach 173

Tomatoes 178

Watermelon 181

Zucchini 187

CHAPTER 8 - How to Defend Against Plant Parasites 195

- Pests, prevention, and treatment: Snails 196

Green Caterpillar: Remedies to eliminate the green caterpillar 197
    Prevention 200
Leaflet Miners 202
    Prevention 203
The Cochineal and Coccoidea 204
    Prevention 206
Ants 209
    Prevention 209
Thrips 210
    Prevention 213
Aphids or Plant Lice 214
    Prevention 219
Plant Mites 222
    Prevention 224
White fly 224
    Prevention 232
Pest Prevention in Indoor Farming 235

CONCLUSION 239

Kevin S. Stevenson
RAISED BED GARDENING FOR BEGINNERS

CHAPTER 1 - Garden with Raised Bed

The gardens of raised beds are the saviours of gardeners with poor soil everywhere. The basic idea of a raised bed is that instead of fighting against poor soil conditions, you build above ground, where you have absolute control over the soil texture and ingredients.

The garden of a raised bed is a garden built above your native soil, sometimes incorporating native soil, sometimes not.

These gardens can be contained, for example when you build a wooden or stone structure to keep the bed intact, or they can be freer, with soil and amendments stacked just a few inches. You can plant everything from herbs and vegetables to perennials and shrubs in a raised bed.

When gardening in a raised bed, you can easily control the type of soil. Your beds warm up faster in spring. You will have fewer weeds and easier time to get rid of the weeds that appear. The soil does not compact like an underground bed. But there is one drawback: you must figure out how to fill a high garden bed. And that seems daunting!

Whether you are using native soil or a soil mix, a mixture of soil and compost or something else, we will look at your options. There are many things you can do to fill the raised beds in your gardens!

What is the bed for?

Filling a high bed can be a challenge.

Before you start planning, you will need to decide what your bed is for. After all, some plants have lower roots than other plants. For example, your average red radish will require very little depth, where a daikon radish requires a couple of feet of soil.

If you have an idea of the depth of the root you will grow in each container, you can customize your filler materials to that. For example, someone who is going to have a bed of devout green leafy vegetables only needs 6-8" of high-quality soil on the surface. Native soil or other materials can be used below this to demonstrate mass. But someone who grows carrots will want at least a foot and a half of quality soil.

Drought-resistant plants often have deeper root systems. These deeper roots allow the plant to look lower for the water they need.

Materials for more depth

Caring for a high, round, raised bed is surprisingly easy.

I am a big fan of raised beds made of cold galvanized 22-gauge steel with upholstery. The coating makes them extremely resistant to rust and resist all weather conditions.

The taller your garden bed, the more materials you will need to fill. For example, a raised metal bed has a diameter of 38", or just a couple of inches over 3 feet. It has a depth of 29". Get about eight square feet of space to plant on the surface. But you will need 18 cubic feet of soil to fill it completely.

When you build your bed, you may question the amount of soil you need. So, let us look at the different configurations you can build and determine the amount of soil each occupies to fill it.

Length	Width	Height	Cu. Ft. fill	Cu. Yd. fill
23.6 "	23.6 "	30 "	10 cu. ft.	0,37 cu. Km.
35.4 "	23.6 "	30 "	15 cu. ft.	0,56 cu. Km.
51 "	23.6 "	30 "	22 cu. ft.	0,81 cu. Km.
35.4 "	35.4 "	30 "	23 cu. ft.	0,85 cu. Km.
63 "	23.6 "	30 "	28 cu. ft.	1.04 cu. Km.
51 "	35.4 "	30 "	33 cu. ft.	1.22 cu. Km.

To make a comparison between that and other raised beds, my 4.5 ' x 4.5 ' x 24 " square beds require 40.5 cubic feet of soil or 1.5 cubic yards to fill. These beds are not only sturdy, they offer a large surface area with lower soil requirements than standard homemade wooden garden beds.

How is the bottom of your garden beds?

Raised beds like this can lift your garden to an easy height to work on!

Since you are putting your top-quality soil on the surface, everything underneath will have to drain excess moisture. Avoid using materials such as rocks at the bottom of the raised bed, as this can create an artificial groundwater table that will prevent good drainage. With raised garden beds, drainage is essential.

What constitutes organic materials?

Old, dry wood can create a suitable base layer, as it decomposes under the ground. Wood also retains some moisture, while at the same time allowing the excess to drain easily.

It will take a couple of years to decompose old branches or small trunks, so keep that in mind. We recommend that you avoid planting deeper vegetables in beds full of wood for a while, opting instead for low root plants. Using wood in this way is a variation of a technique called hügelkultur.

Other garden waste products can also make a good base layer. Cuttings of grass, dried leaves or leaf mould, clippings from other plants and the like can fill the bottom of the bed. These will quickly break down in the soil, increasing the organic content of the soil. However, as they decompose, they will lose height and you will see clear signs of the soil level falling towards the end of the season. This is still an excellent way to start a brand-new raised bed, as you can continue building the ground later.

Do you have a pile of compost that has not been demolished yet? Put that half-finished compost on the bottom of a bed. It will keep collapsing in there. You can mix some local garden soil with it if you want, but you do not have to. These lower layers are also great places to bury your bokashi, supplementing it with grass clippings and other garden waste before adding soil.

Custom blends

You can buy a mixture of land from a landscape architecture company to fill your beds, but it can be prohibitive and messy. It is eight cubic yards of land in a pile about 4' high with a footprint of 12'x20'. If you do not need depth, fill with more material!

Now that your base is full and you are ready to add your growing layer, it is time to consider what you actually want to plant in. This is the top layer of your garden bed, raised above any filler material you have chosen. And it is from this top layer that your plants will absorb most of their nutrients and water.

A common raised soil mix is known as Mel's Mix. This mix consists of equal parts peat moss and coarse vermiculite. This mix is wonderful for most raised beds, but only if the bed is on a surface that drains well. If you were building your raised bed on concrete or hard clay, you might want to opt for a more draining mix. Adding perlite to this mix can help improve drainage. If you prefer to use something sustainable, rice hulls are great substitutes for perlite.

When I started my beds, I went with a custom mix. My top layers were a mixture of composted dairy products and chicken manure, leaf and plant compost, sandy soil, aged forest humus, peat moss, wheat straw and shielded local soil. This worked wonderfully, but due to the high levels of organic material, it lost almost a third of its height in the first year when it broke down.

One question many people have is whether there is a "perfect" mix for raised beds. It depends on how your climate is and which plants you will grow. You can use a bagged plant mix that is presumably designed for raised beds and will work. But depending on the climate, it may or may not be "perfect" for you.

The prepared mixes do not retain enough moisture to keep my plants alive during my torrid summers. If you are in an area where it rains a lot or it is cold, you will probably want extra drainage. Improve and customize your soil to work with your climate and needs!

If you grow food crops, there is another question that needs to be answered. The food crops you are growing could be heavy feeders. The garden soil for these will need a lot of manure or fertilizer. I like compacted milk manure and worm castings mixed with peat or coconut moss and some local soil. With quality compost, you may not need to add fertilizer for the next season.

Annual supply of the raised bed

Every autumn I pick and mow the leaves with a lawnmower. Leaf mulch is an exceptional material to complete the bed space.

Every autumn I harvest all the fallen leaves that I can find, destroy them with my lawnmower and make a deep mulch in all the beds that are not active. The worms in my soil break many leaves during the winter and create a lovely soil surface and humus that my plants love. Leaf moulds like this are one of the best organic additions you can make to your raised garden beds.

Consider making your raised bed in the fall using a layered method. Make sure you layer fresh green materials between dry brown materials. For example, alfalfa hay, plant waste or grass residues are green, while dried straw, thin wood chips or dried leaves are brown. Make a layer of brown, then a layer of green and, if you wish, add a layer of manure to complete it. Repeat this layering until you reach the top of the bed. You may also want to mount it slightly above the surface of the bed. By spring, you will have a nice surface to plant on and help you fill your beds.

I use a variation of the lasagne method using specially chosen ingredients. I select materials with a high nitrogen content such as alfalfa hay and certified hen manure without weed seeds and layer them between dry leaves and pine chips. Once I have accumulated 6" to 8" stratified materials, I add it with about 3" of compost manure, then "put it to bed" covering the bed surface with something to prevent weed seeds from entering. The landscape fabric is effective enough for this purpose.

When spring comes, I remove the horizontal fabric cover. There will still be a couple of inches of material that has not completely decomposed, often dulled under the surface of the manure. I use the tip of a trowel to drill holes in this opaque layer and plant in the hole. If not, do not modify the opaque layer, as it works extremely well to keep the soil moist. This way every autumn, you will significantly improve the yield for your plants in spring.

Don't you want to try composting in your raised garden beds? That is fine. You can simply add more soil and compost if necessary, the following year. I like to add coconut or peat moss for better moisture retention. If I need more drainage, I will add perlite or rice hulls.

The use of mulch with wood chips during the growing season will act as a form of composting. As time goes by, the fine wood chips will break up, increasing the mass of the soil. They will also fall into the soil, providing additional drainage capacity.

I hope I have given you the inspiration for ways to fill your larger raised beds. I know it can be a challenge, but those bigger beds are worth the effort.

CHAPTER 2 - How to Grow on Raised Beds

Many times both in vegetable gardens and in gardens one of the longest and most complex operations is to differentiate the soil according to the planting species; flowering plants but also vegetables and evergreens have, for each species, different needs, and being able to "follow them" means always having beautiful plants and productive gardens.

The technique of cultivation on raised beds has first of all just the purpose and the right structural characteristics to allow this differentiation and to do it with absolute simplicity, giving you the opportunity to vary the soil according to the specific needs of your plants, so it will be easy to get a bed for plants that love acid soil, another one for those who prefer a basic soil, or little irrigation and so on; fertilizing also specifically and without waste.

Basically, this style of cultivation consists in raising the soil for the specific planting (bed), compared to the surrounding soil, and to delimit the various cultivations using wooden planks, rather than bricks or tiles.

But the advantages of this method of cultivation are really many; for example, the fact that avoiding to step on the cultivated area when working it or simply when doing maintenance or harvesting, just because it is raised compared to the working soil, you avoid compacting it allowing a greater inflow of air that the roots need so much.

Another not inconsiderable advantage is the increase in productivity obtained thanks to the fact that the plants can stay close to each other, since it is not necessary to provide passage land, and in this way the problem of weed growth is also greatly limited, thus reducing maintenance in general.

Moreover, with this technique it is possible to cultivate even if you have a garden with an unsuitable soil, because by raising it you can obtain an area with soil composed specifically for your plant, which in addition will have a better drainage because it is raised compared to the compact soil below in which water stagnations form (also harmful for the proliferation of fungal diseases and parasite attacks).

Finally, by growing on raised beds, in the case of vegetables, you will have the possibility of extending the cultivation over time, and increasing production accordingly, since raised beds heat up earlier in spring and remain productive for a longer period.

RAISED BED GARDENING FOR BEGINNERS

The creation of raised beds is really simple, all you need to do is raise the ground at least 15/20 cm; a lower height is not recommended, while a higher one will be useful to avoid bending down during gardening work and therefore much more comfortable.

The length of the bed is optional and conditioned only by what you want to achieve, what you want to grow and how much you want to extend this cultivation. As far as width is concerned, it is advisable that it is wide enough to allow at least two rows of plants to be planted. Be careful, however, not to exaggerate in width so as not to run the risk of not reaching the centre of the bed when you must harvest or maintain it.

As far as the delimitation of the beds is concerned, the only trick, in case you decide to use wood and make your own border perimeter, is to periodically pass two coats of protective impregnation to the wooden planks so that they can better withstand the weather and the various climatic conditions and, in the case of reclaimed planks, pay attention to any potentially dangerous nails or screws.

It is possible to find on the market, at any garden centre, predefined kits that include connection joints and hinges, so that you can configure the shape and height of the bed whatever your space and needs.

Kevin S. Stevenson
RAISED BED GARDENING FOR BEGINNERS

CHAPTER 3 - How to Build a Raised Bed, Step by Step

The advantages of cultivation on raised beds are really many; first, with this technique it will be much easier to differentiate the soil according to the needs of the plant, compared to the classic cultivation on the ground.

Opting for this type of cultivation will also make it much more convenient and quicker to work the soil and carry out all maintenance operations, you can drastically reduce the problem of weeds and, avoiding to compact the soil with the trampling, you will also allow a better flow of air and water to the roots of the plants.

Another important advantage is that by deciding to cultivate our vegetables, rather than aromatic herbs or flowering plants, by using the technique of raised beds it will be possible to do it also on the balcony, on the terrace or maybe in an area of the garden previously unused because it lacks a soil with the right characteristics.

Basically, this cultivation technique consists in raising the soil for the plants and delimiting the different cultivations through the realization of simple structures obtained by assembling wooden planks rather than bricks or stones of various kinds.

Let us see how to realize a functional raised bed in a few simple moves.

Materials needed and Procedure

- 4 wooden planks 10 x 10 x 40 cm
- 2 wooden boards 5 x 30 x 120 cm
- 2 wooden boards 5 x 30 x 240 cm
- 24 wood screws 8,5 cm
- 24 wood screws 1,5 cm
- 6 PVC pipes with 20 mm diameter and 30 mm length
- 6 metal pipe fittings

We start the construction by assembling a 120 cm board with a square axis. It may be useful to use a retainer to temporarily hold the pieces together before inserting the screws.

So that the wood does not weaken, it is advisable to drill before fastening the screws.

Three screws for each board and three for each corner will be enough. Always make sure that the boards are aligned at the bottom with the square blocks.

At this point we should turn the bed and look for the best position for the final installation; the chosen area must have at least 6 hours of sun exposure per day.

We should anchor the bed on the floor making a hole of about 12-15 cm for each foot.

Once this is done, it is necessary to check that the bed is in bubble, i.e. level, so that the irrigation water can distribute evenly in the ground, without causing stagnation.

Now it is time to install the PVC pipes, three for each side panel of the bed. The pipes will be fixed inside the bed using the metal hooks; these pipes have the function of support for the positioning of the net that will be added to the structure to protect our small bird garden and from the cold.

At this point we will prepare a mixture of soil and compost and distribute it throughout the bed taking care to moisten it well.

You can add a drip irrigation system by inserting a pipe along the wide side of the bed and another 4 for the length, as you can see in the photo.

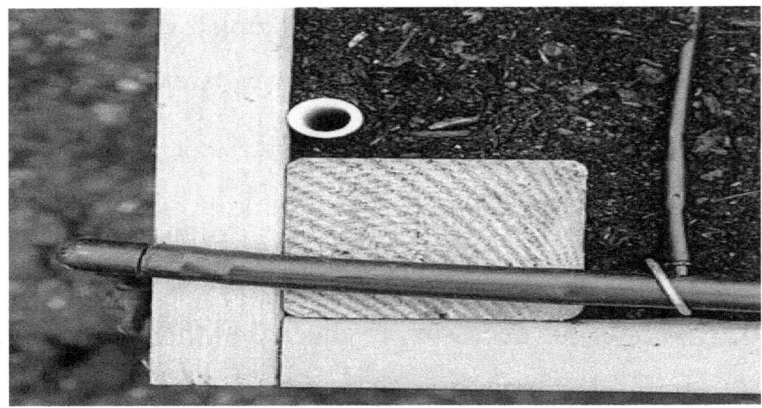

Now it will be possible to grow what we want, create a small vegetable garden rather than a delightful flowering area.

Finally, by attaching other curved PVC pipes to the PVC pipes it will be possible to create a sort of protection using a plastic sheet, and thus transforming our raised bed into a small greenhouse.

Create a vegetable garden inside pots and vases

The procedure for cultivating a small vegetable garden inside pots or vases is very similar - in many ways - to that illustrated above for growing in wooden boxes. Line the containers with black mylar sheets, then place a layer of expanded clay on the bottom, to drain the water well, then create a mix of peat, soil and vermiculite, perlite or sand - in equal parts - and use it to fill the pots used, taking care to leave 2-3 centimetres free from the edge.

Once this is done, irrigate the soil abundantly, then leave it to rest for a few hours to create the ideal conditions for sowing. Plant the seeds according to the instructions on the package and - since not all seeds germinate - plant more than necessary. After sowing, water gently - but abundantly - to allow the seed to sink deep down and stabilise in the soil.

After this step, you must ensure that your potted garden is watered regularly and thoroughly: to avoid making mistakes, regularly check your plants and the moisture level of the soil and - if you find it is too dry - add water.

To ensure that the soil is properly hydrated, it is preferable to have a drip irrigation system so that you can schedule watering and make sure that you provide your plants with the right amount of water, provided, of course, that you regularly check the condition of the soil. About 30 days after sowing, water your plants with a water-soluble fertilizer, following the instructions on the package. Of course, one of the weekly tasks is to control weeds and keep pests away, although potted or potted crops - just like those in raised gardens - are less susceptible to pests and diseases. In any case, it is necessary to control them and eradicate any problems.

Kevin S. Stevenson
RAISED BED GARDENING FOR BEGINNERS

CHAPTER 4 – Raised garden in 6 easy steps

After having made a wooden box in very few moves as seen in the previous chapter, let us go deeper into the subject and see what the steps are to get a working raised garden.

The characteristic of the raised garden is the structure of the flowerbed which is not at ground level but raised from the ground. This gives us the possibility to manage a tidier vegetable garden but above all to cultivate it even on poorly fertile, stony ground or even on the balcony.

These garden chests, in addition to be a decorative element for the landscape, offer other advantages. For example, they make cultivation less tiring, simplifying the management of weeds and pests. They also potentially increase the yield of the crop.

If you are already thinking of enjoying the taste of your harvest, do not forget to follow these valuable tips.

Let us discover together how to build a raised garden in 6 simple steps:

1. **Choosing the right building materials.** Before you start building your own raised garden, it is important to decide which materials you will use to build it. Although

materials such as: heavy wood, rail crossbars and concrete blocks are more resistant than others, it is better to use something lighter and more practical. The advice is to use thin wood panels, which are lighter. Once they are full, the boxes will still be rather heavy but easier to move if necessary.

2. **Respect the measurements.** The idea behind a raised garden is that you can build a simple and easily accessible space. Therefore, it is necessary to create a flowerbed that is not too large. According to experts, the ideal size is 120 cm wide for a medium-sized person. In this way you can easily reach the centre of the box from both sides without hindrance.

3. **How to keep out weeds.** Another problem to keep in mind are weeds. In fact, weeds are a common nuisance in all cultivated areas. So, in order to prevent weeds from climbing up from the ground through the weeds, you only need to build a barrier to prevent it. To do this, you need to lay a thick layer of cardboard on the ground or on the grass at the base of the box, covering every space carefully. This quick solution will prevent the seeds of germinating weeds from contaminating your raised garden.

4. **What you must add to the soil.** Once you have made the potting box and placed the cardboard against weeds, it is time to fill it with potting soil. Always use good quality

soil and to save a little on costs add a layer of dead leaves or cut grass. As well as saving you something on the cost of the soil, these organic materials will decompose over time and thus enrich the soil with nutrients.

5. **Protect the raised garden**. Another important piece of advice is to arrange cover sheets for the rows and nets for the birds. Then, before completely filling the box, you should insert vertically placed PVC pipe segments along the inside walls of the container. When it is time to cover the plants, you will have to put the ends of the supporting structures for the sheets inside the pipes.

6. **Autumn mulching**. Throughout the autumn period it will be important to remove any plant residues from the raised bed and sprinkle the soil with a layer of mulch of about 5-8 cm. If you do not want to buy it in the shop you can use what you have in the garden as an alternative, such as dead leaves or cut grass. The mulch will keep the soil moist during the winter, as well as releasing nutrients during decomposition.

Kevin S. Stevenson
RAISED BED GARDENING FOR BEGINNERS

CHAPTER 5 – 10 Ideas for Making a Functional and Aesthetic Raised Bed

The construction of a raised garden can be a very good idea as well as a very bad idea, let us try to see the pros and cons.

The first thing we must try to understand is why we should focus on this solution and whether it is indispensable for us.

It is a fact that a raised garden is generally more orderly and aesthetically pleasing, but this has little to do with the cultivation and growth of vegetables.

But let us take a step back: what is meant by a raised garden?

It is quite simple, they are plots, mostly dedicated to individual crops, which are raised above ground level.

The raised flowerbeds can be in masonry, wood, plastic, they can be high and can be equipped with mulch sheets, irrigation systems, etc.

Structures for a Raised Garden

I think that a raised garden is a particularly expensive and impractical solution in many cases.

Everything depends, of course, on the material used to create the flowerbeds and support the soil but, in general, in addition to the cost of materials there is a fair amount of work to be done, as much greater as the structures will be considered fixed and high.

It is true that to create the raised perimeter of the plots you can also reuse materials that you are already at home (planks of wood, pieces of sheet metal, stones), but it is also true that if you do not want to transform your garden into an agglomeration resembling a slum, you need a certain consistency of materials, which means having to buy them.

As mentioned above, a raised vegetable garden can be incredibly beautiful to look at, but if the materials are heterogeneous, this beauty risks turning into landscape degradation.

Why create a raised garden?

The reasons may be different, from that of an aesthetic nature, as mentioned above, to that of a practical nature, as we shall see.

A vegetable garden is a vegetable garden and in it, by definition, vegetables and some fruit are grown.

Now, the main reason why it may be interesting to build raised flowerbeds is the poor quality of the soil.

Often you must deal with heavy soils where water stagnates or, conversely, with sandy and arid soils with few nutrients and where water runs off very quickly.

Correcting these types of soil is not extremely easy and therefore raised caissons can be made where a soil suitable for growing most vegetables can be created.

If you go further, you can even create pots with slightly different soils depending on the type of plant you are going to grow there.

Which material to choose for the structure of the raised garden?

The choice of materials is especially important because the raised flowerbeds of the garden will have to remain in their place for a long time.

Personally, I do not recommend the creation of fixed masonry structures in order to always leave the possibility to change, one day, or dismantle everything, without great difficulty.

This does not detract from the fact that it is possible to use dry masonry structures which, being easy to build, can also be dismantled with the same ease.

By raised masonry gardens I mean, therefore, dry-stone structures that are not bound with cement mortar.

We can consider them as semi-permanent structures which, compared to wooden structures, require in any case a much greater effort.

Let us now see some materials and possible structures for the raised garden.

Wooden chests

Wooden planks are the easiest way to create a raised flowerbed.

The variable, in these rectangular or square structures, consists of the 4 posts to anchor the planks.

In one case the support poles, strictly square or triangular in section, can be fixed inside the perimeter of the box and the planks will then be nailed to the poles.

This is the simplest and most aesthetically pleasing solution because on the outside we only see the boards and the support poles are not an obstacle.

This solution is particularly suitable in case of low raised flowerbeds.

The other possibility is to fix 8 poles, 2 for each corner, outside the structure.

In this way the planks do not have to be nailed down but will remain in place thanks to the thrust of the soil that will be placed inside the box.

The support poles placed outside are visually less pleasant and can be a hindrance.

The poles should always be firmly planted in the ground to support the structure.

A third possibility, for those who are more experienced in carpentry work, is to fit the boards together, but even then, we have some overhangs that I personally do not appreciate.

In the latter case the structure is self-supporting and there is no need for poles.

Masonry raised garden

With bricks I indicate here the classic solid bricks, terracotta, or perforated bricks that have a certain thickness.

These are, in all cases, perfectly regular elements that can be placed, alternating courses, one on top of the other to obtain dry-stone walls.

If the raised flowerbeds were particularly low, the bricks could simply be aligned vertically by burying half of their length in the ground.

On how to make a brick wall we have already written an article that we recommend you read, even if it refers to bricks bound with mortar the bricks could still be laid dry following a certain pattern.

If the raised flowerbed has a certain height, the bricks should be laid in such a way that the short side remains visible and the structure is more solid and thicker.

Gabions to fill with stones

If you think that metal gabions are used exclusively for road containment works, you are mistaken.

Gabions are not only those cyclopean structures that we often imagine, as they have been put on the market much more slender structures suitable for a variety of purposes.

What they have in common with their ancestors is that they are metal gabions, with large meshes, which must be filled with stones.

The advantage of these cages to create a raised garden is that, once the cage is installed, you can use a material at no cost such as stones, perhaps even reclaiming a particularly stony ground.

Also, in this case, just as for wooden and masonry structures, the internal part of the structure should be covered with a cloth to contain the soil.

More reason, in this case, the retaining sheet is indispensable to prevent it from filtering through the stones.

That of stone gabions is not a particularly economical solution, but neither is it more expensive than a drywall, of the same size, made with bricks.

The result is aesthetically pleasing and the cages with the stones can be dismantled and reassembled elsewhere.

Nothing prohibits, of course, to create low dry-stone walls, but the work would be quite heavy and, in the absence of stones a bit squared, even difficult to achieve.

Pallet

By recycling an old pallet, it is possible to create a raised bed perfect for any area of the garden or vegetable garden, it is a quite simple and above all economical project.

Old Furniture

Even old furniture, rather than parts of furniture components, lends itself well to making a raised bed. In this case the result is magnificent and, placed in a vegetable garden, this structure can transform it into an elegant and original place.

Earthenware Pots

With a good number of earthenware vases an ecstatic and practical edging has been created, which acts as a raised bed; a way to make the most of the cultivable space and to recycle old vases, rather than other containers.

Aluminium bathtub

An aluminium tub has been reused as a large and modern container, a raised bed and at the same time a truly original vase.

Pneumatic Tires

Recycling is always a great way to start creative projects that are really appealing; some of the end-of-life tyres have been turned into original raised beds in which you can grow vegetables, fruits, or ornamental plants.

Cement blocks

In this case, perforated concrete blocks have been recycled to create a round raised bed, inside which a spiral of flowers grown on sloping soil has been created; the decorative effect is very striking.

Special shape

Finally, in this case, using wood, a raised bed with a particular shape has been created, ideal for growing flowering species mixed with vegetables and small shrubs; if you want you can also use other materials, change the shape and create a large flowerbed really original.

The advantages of a raised garden

The main advantage is, essentially, to be able to improve the soil without having to operate on the entire surface of the garden.

From an aesthetic point of view, it is an appreciable solution, the garden is cleaner and tidier.

With raised flowerbeds it is more difficult for animals such as snails to attack the crops, especially if we spread wood ash at the base of the beds.

The raised garden tends to heat up more quickly, favouring the germination and development of plants, especially in the middle seasons.

If the flowerbeds are raised enough it will greatly benefit the back and, as written above, even people with some motor disabilities can, quite easily, devote themselves to this hobby in the open air.

The soil, not being compacted by the continuous trampling, is on average crumblier and therefore suitable for the development of the root system of the plants.

The plants get a little lighter than the ground level and this also favours their development.

Now we come to the disadvantages, which are not lacking.

The disadvantages of the Raised Garden

The work to be done to build a raised garden is not indifferent, both from the point of view of the construction of the actual structure and the subsequent filling with earth.

The raised garden is quite expensive because to improve the quality of the soil you need to buy bags of soil, manure, etc.

The space between the caissons is substantially unused and, in any case, must be large enough to comfortably turn a wheelbarrow or a lawn mower.

Forget that you can use a tiller in a raised flowerbed, so the soil must be tilled by hand.

Raised coffers accumulate heat but also give it away quickly, so providing adequate mulching of the surface is highly recommended.

The higher the beds are raised, the more difficult it is to integrate drip irrigation systems.

Raised chests, if made of untreated wood, tend to rot over time.

After filling the caissons with soil, you have to wet them and wait for them to settle a little bit, as the loose soil has a larger volume but then tends to shrink, so wait a moment before planting the plants.

CHAPTER 6 - What's the Point of Planting?

Deciding what to plant in a vegetable garden is much easier than you might think. If you plan it all carefully, you will be able to enjoy a beautiful green space, rich in vegetables, without having to spend hours and hours working on it.

If you are starting to grow for the first time, it is advisable to start small and then expand as you go along and only after you have learned and acquired the basics. The risk, in fact, is to plant many more plants than you really need for your family's needs, an aspect that makes your garden difficult to manage, both from the point of view of the care to devote and the quantity of the harvest.

The plants that generally offer abundant fruit are tomatoes, peppers and courgettes, because they continue to produce throughout the summer; on the contrary, vegetables such as carrots, radishes and maize produce only once and - in this case - it is probably necessary to provide for a higher number of plants. As we have seen in the previous chapters, creating a vegetable garden and taking care of it is not that difficult, but if you decide to start today it is appropriate to go step by step, starting with plants that are simpler to manage, and then try your hand at more complex ones, which require more care and time. Among the most suitable plants for beginners we recommend arugula and

"Soncino" (valerian), but also radishes and carrots, which - as we have seen - are plants that produce only once, however they are perfect to start experimenting with the world of the garden.

The rocket, for example, should be planted from mid-March onwards (after the period of frost and the great winter cold): after cleaning and tilling the soil carefully, sow the rocket in holes, about half a centimetre deep, and spaced - one from the other - about 10-12 centimetres apart. Water regularly every day, at the end of the day or early in the morning, and within 7-10 days you will see the first seedlings appear.

Before picking it, you will have to wait about 30-35 days and - when cutting it - remember not to cut everything, but to leave a few centimetres from the ground, so that it can grow again.

If, on the other hand, you have decided to grow valerian, you can sow it from the middle of August to the beginning of November, following the same scheme indicated above for the rocket: create furrows half a centimetre deep, about 10 centimetres apart and then sow, taking care to irrigate correctly, so that the soil is always damp.

After a few days, you will see the seedlings sprout, which you can harvest after about 15 days. Always remember to keep the soil clean, removing weeds.

And now let us come to carrots, quite easy to grow, healthy - because they are rich in vitamins - and always precious and useful in the kitchen for many different preparations. Carrots, like rocket and valerian, are also quite easy to grow and can withstand very different temperatures, which is why they grow very well everywhere. In places where the temperatures are lower, they are sown indicatively (much depends also on the microclimate of the area) between the months of March and June, while in places where the temperatures are higher, they are sown between February and May.

The soil must be cleaned and worked creating furrows about 25 centimetres deep and removing anything that may disturb the growth and development of the roots, such as stones, roots of other plants, wooden sticks, etc. This does not exist if you have prepared the soil in the way described above. Once you have prepared the soil, you must proceed with sowing: insert the seeds in the grooves you have prepared, leaving a space of 25 cm between one and the other.

Pay attention to the cleanliness of the soil and you will be able to harvest your carrots about 4 months after sowing.

Regardless of the type of plants you decide to grow, always remember that taking care of and keeping your small garden clean and healthy also means obtaining a higher production; in short: a well-kept space of 5 X 5 meters is able to produce more than a 25x50 meters growing area, therefore considerably larger, but full of weeds or sick plants.

What to plant in the garden: the calendar month by month

What to plant in January?

The first thing to do with the start of the new year is to remove the residues of the plants grown the previous year from the ground. Then, depending on the climate and the areas in which you are located, you can start cultivating:

- in a warm bed (in a small greenhouse) or under glass: summer cabbage, aubergines, tomatoes, peppers, radishes, celery, melons, watermelons, lettuces.
- in the open field, instead, you can plant white garlic, proceed with the sowing of broad beans and peas.

What to plant in February?

In February we proceed with the sowing of the vegetables which we will then harvest in spring/summer. This operation follows the sowing calendar which in turn is influenced by the moon phases.

- With the waning moon, the leafy vegetables and celery are sown under shelter and the chard, spinach and lettuce are planted.
- with the waning moon, on the other hand, carrots, radishes, and peas are usually fertilised in the open air and aromatic herbs are grown under shelter.

What to sow in March?

What to sow in March depends very much on the type of climate. It can happen that if you sow too early and there are sudden drops in temperature or excessive rainfall, the entire harvest is lost.

In general, however, March is the right month to plant:

- in protected crops: watermelon, basil, artichokes, head cabbage, cabbage, cucumber, endives, fennel, aubergines, peppers, tomatoes, leeks, celery, zucchini, and herbs.
- in the open field: garden beets, beets, carrots, cut chicory, onions, lettuces, peas, parsley, turnips, radishes, rocket, spinach.

April, what to plant in the garden

During the month of April you can plant: watermelons, asparagus, basil, chard and ribs, artichokes, thistles, carrots, cabbage, chicory, onions, endives, beans, green beans, fennel, salad, melons, aubergines, peppers, peas, parsley, radishes, rocket, celery, zucchini.

Moreover, by the 10th of the month you can plant the chickpeas and after the 25th of the month proceed with the sowing of the potato.

May, what to plant in the garden

The plants to sow in May include beans, green beans, peppers, aubergines, zucchini, Brussels sprouts, cucumbers, strawberries.

A small caution: in May temperatures tend to rise, so it is necessary to water in the early hours of the morning and after sunset in order to prevent excessive temperature changes from withering the plants.

June, what to plant in the garden

June is the month of beets, basil, carrot, chard, cabbage, chicory, beans, lettuce, leek, parsley, radish, rocket, celery, zucchini.

Attention must also be paid to fungal diseases and insect attacks on the already developed plants of tomatoes, aubergines, and peppers. It is also necessary to prepare supports and nets for climbing plants and clean the tomatoes from unnecessary growing parts.

The garden in July and August

In July and August, basil, chard, carrot, cauliflower, chicory, onions, endive, fennel, fennel, beans, green beans, lettuce, parsley, radish, turnips, rocket, valerian, courgettes are sown in the open field.

Considering that we are in the hottest months of the year it is good to water regularly and carry out all the operations to control weeds and diseases that can attack the plant.

In August you can start to arrange the soil for subsequent transplanting of chicory, cabbage, cabbage, tomatoes, fennel.

What to plant in the garden in September?

September is the right month to sow beets, chard, carrot, cabbage, chicory, endives, fennel, lettuce, parsley, turnips, radishes, rocket, spinach, valerian.

October: what is in the garden

With the arrival of autumn and colder temperatures it becomes more difficult to know what to plant in the garden, because there are fewer varieties of plants that are suitable for this season. Usually, chicory, broad beans, lettuce, parsley, radish, rocket, spinach, and valerian are sown in the open field. October is also the right month for sowing peas and planting onions.

November and December

In these months' beans, peas, radishes, spinach, and valerian are sown in the open field. While they are grown in warm beds or under glass lettuce, green chicory, rocket. In addition, throughout the month of November and until the first 15 days of December, peas and onion and garlic bulbs can still be planted.

CHAPTER 7 – Plant Profiles

Vertical Strawberry Growing

The fact that our gardens are getting smaller and smaller, especially in the city, is a fact and then you must be clever.

Vertical cultivation is not new, but neither is it so much exploited outside of professional cultivation.

Cultivating vertically means making the most of the little space available, especially for those crops whose root system does not need deep soil to expand.

Strawberries are among the most suitable plants to be grown vertically, and in this article, we will give examples of some systems for doing so.

In fact, ground cultivation of strawberries has its drawbacks:

- Strawberry offshoots, if not controlled, tend to colonise the ground, covering practically the entire useful surface area.
- in order to ensure the best healthiness of the fruit, they should not come into direct contact with the soil.

- Therefore, it is necessary to mulch the soil or spread special sheets before planting.
- strawberry plants grown on the ground occupy considerable space despite having a modest root system.
- during the ripening period of the strawberries you find yourself with large quantities of fruit and the harvesting on the ground turns into a nightmare for the spine.

For all these reasons, and for others that I may have omitted, vertical cultivation is a solution that should be taken seriously.

Cultivating strawberries vertically, and not only, means saving space and effort during harvesting, but also saving many interventions that are generally related to ground cultivation: insect infestation, mold generation, etc.

The advice, however, is always to focus on re-flowering plants that guarantee a prolonged production rather than one concentrated in just two/three weeks. With strawberries you can eat these juicy fruits from May until late autumn (weather permitting).

Growing in big baskets

Who among us has never received a gift basket containing so many delicacies at Christmas or Easter?

After the holidays these baskets, usually wicker, end up being thrown away also because they are quite voluminous.

Well, perhaps it is the case to keep them to grow strawberries inside them, hanging them at human height in our garden.

Obviously, it is necessary to insert inside the basket a plastic cloth in order to avoid that the soil does not come out from the possible cracks, that the water does not disperse too quickly and that the basket, in contact with the water, does not rot.

Growing in old gutters

Old gutters can be filled with soil and strawberry plants can find their place there.

The gutters can be hung on a wall that is well exposed to the sun and arranged horizontally or slightly inclined so that excess water does not stagnate but flows out of the gutters on the upper floors into the lower floors.

Vertical growing in PVC pipes

Sometimes it happens to have large diameter PVC pipes after the construction of a new house.

Often these pipes end up being stored somewhere not knowing what to do with them. In the worst cases they end up being thrown away.

By placing the PVC pipes vertically, almost like towers, it is possible to grow strawberries in them.

To do this, it is necessary to create numerous alternate holes on the pipe and then, starting from the bottom, fill the pipe with soil and, once at the level of the hole, place a strawberry plant.

Continue in this way until the tube is filled.

The holes that we are going to create with a hole cutter must not be too wide to prevent the soil from escaping.

The irrigation will be done from above by fall.

Strawberries grown in pots

Aluminium pots are found in all kitchens. At best they end up being thrown into the glass bell and sent for recycling.

Aluminium is a safe material in which many foods are stored. We can then recycle some cans ourselves and then grow our own plants inside them and hang them in the garden like little lanterns.

Of course, their capacity is limited and so is the soil they can contain. In theory, even strawberry, although not very demanding, would need more space to expand its root system.

We can make up for this lack of soil and, consequently, for a lower availability of nutrients, by making regular liquid fertilizations.

The cans should be drilled into the bottom with a nail and a hammer to allow the excess water to drain off.

Arugula

It is a very simple plant to grow and productive, so it is a recommended cultivation of the organic family garden. From the point of view of adversities, it often happens to find the leaves pierced by eltica and other small insects, which do more aesthetic damage than substance. The beauty of this crop is that it is very rustic and therefore can be kept for a good part of the year, also has a short cultivation cycle, so from sowing to harvesting the step is short.

Suitable climate. The rocket is very adaptable and for this reason it is particularly easy to put in the garden. Like many other crops in the garden, it is afraid of water stagnation, which encourages it to become sick, and drought, which can cause it to grow early to seed. The frosts can damage it, but it resists well to the cold, bearing temperatures up to 5 degrees.

The ideal soil. Any type of soil is good for growing rocket, with preference for a soil which is draining but rich in organic substance, not tending to dry up with the heat.

Sowing period. The rocket can be sown from March to September, however, with tunnel cultivation it is possible to extend the growing period and have this fresh salad available for harvesting practically all year round. The rocket seeds last a long time: you can use a packet of seeds bought during the year for up to 4 years. The arugula germinates quickly and has a rapid growth: a week after sowing you will already see the seedlings sprout and after a short time you can harvest the first leaves to put in the salad.

Sixth of planting or sowing by spreading. The arugula can be sown easily in rows. The sowing is faster, you throw the seeds and then rake them lightly, to cover them with soil. Sowing by rows, on the other hand, has the advantage of a better distribution of the plants, which remain well ventilated. In this case, you must keep 25 cm between the rows and 5/10 cm between the seedlings. The seed must be buried at a shallow depth, even half a centimetre is enough.

Irrigations. The rocket requires frequent irrigation after sowing and until the seedlings take root, afterwards it becomes a little more tolerant. In any case, if the rains do not intervene, it is still a plant to wet. Irrigation on the rocket should be done often but with little water, it does not like large amounts of water, but it is necessary to water frequently to keep the soil moist. Same philosophy to make the rocket grow on the balcony, compared to the garden, however, the cultivation in pots needs an even more regular supply of water.

Weeding. Hoeing is necessary, both to keep the soil airy and to keep it clean from weeds and weeds, which, if they develop a lot, can suffocate the plants of wrinkles.

Diseases and pests. Rococles fear nettles, small soil lice that pierce the leaves of the rocket and generally attack the cruciferous. Apart from these soil fleas, they are quite resistant plants, also thanks to their short cycle. If they are planted well-spaced, they are not afraid of fungal diseases, so on naturally moist soils it is better to choose to sow by row rather than by spreading.

Harvest the rocket

The arugula leaves can also be picked immediately, obviously it is better to wait for the plant to be strong enough to be able to vegetate again without difficulty, so it generally expects the leaves to reach 7-8 cm in height. This height is usually reached in about a month after sowing, which is an ideal time to start harvesting.

The young leaves are the tenderest, while growing they become a little leatherier. To harvest you cut the leaf near the collar, a plant can harvest even 5-6 times, then continue to harvest.

Asparagus

The asparagus plant is cultivated for several years.

In order to grow it in the vegetable garden, it is necessary to create an asparagus plant, which is maintained for about ten years and is quite cumbersome in terms of space, so the crop is not very suitable for small urban gardens.

Asparagus takes a few years to enter production, so it is not harvested in the year of planting as with most garden vegetables. It is therefore a bit laborious to start growing asparagus, but it is certainly worth it: it is a vegetable with extraordinary organoleptic characteristics and excellent nutritional properties and it is a great satisfaction to see the asparagus "shoots" grow robust and luxuriant.

Ideal climate. The asparagus plant prefers a climate without excessive cold or even heat, but it is quite resistant and versatile.

The position of the flowerbed should be well sunny and not too exposed to the wind.

The space required. As a precondition for growing asparagus, it should be specified that it requires a lot of space. Even for a production intended for family consumption, several square metres of occupied vegetable garden should be considered.

The right soil. One of the main soils and climate requirements for asparagus is a well-drained soil. If the soil is clayey or not very loose, it can be mixed with sand to make it lighter and more suitable for asparagus growing. Drainage can be helped by studying a suitable system (drainage channels or raised flowerbeds such as baulatura).

Fertilisation. It is important that the planting is well-fertilised to enrich the soil so that it can withstand several years of asparagus cultivation. It is advisable to use mature compost or manure, in any case organic fertilisers must be used for organic cultivation.

Sowing. Asparagus can be grown from the so-called 'legs' or from seed. The legs can be bought in the garden, but they are generally quite expensive, although they make cultivation quicker and easier.

Start with asparagus seed. If you start from the seed you plant at the beginning of spring, to transplant then to formed seedling. Asparagus plants should be planted in the soil when the climate is already warm (usually in June).

Start with the legs. The famous legs are the rhizomes of the asparagus plant, which can be found in any nursery or garden centre. The legs are buried in the ground in early spring: from February (warm areas) and throughout March and April.

Flat or slatted planting. Being a plant that lasts several years, asparagus justifies the work of creating raised flowerbeds, to facilitate the flow of water and avoid dangerous stagnation during the rainiest periods. Where the soil is by nature draining, it is not necessary to intervene with "baulature", but where it is not, it is advisable to cultivate asparagus by raising the flowerbeds.

Sixth of planting. The asparagus is a cumbersome plant, as a sixth of planting it is necessary to give a good distance between the rows. Usually one metre between one row and the other and about 35 cm between one plant and the other along the row.

How to plant asparagus. When planting asparagus it is better to dig about 30 cm and deposit a thick layer of mature manure, in the absence of manure you can use compost, also excellent humus. Above the manure a small layer of soil on which you put the legs of asparagus, which are then covered with earth (surface layer). If we have the seedlings we proceed in the same way with the compost, then instead of burying the legs we transplant them. If you want to make a raised flowerbed it is better instead of digging to make a mound that has the same elements (manure, earth, paws, soil). After the implantation of the paws or the transplanting of the seedlings you wet the soil well to stimulate the rooting.

The asparagus growing cycle

<u>First year of cultivation:</u>

February-March: If you want to start with the seed, you plant it in trays.

February-April: if you start from the legs you plant.

June: for those who have made or bought asparagus seedlings, they are planted in the garden.

From June: normal cultivation operations (weeding to avoid weeds, irrigation if necessary). Do not touch the shoots for the whole first year: the plants must develop and bloom.

Autumn (October): cut the yellowed stems and spread a layer (3-4 cm) of mature manure or compost. This protects the plants and their root system from frost, as well as providing nutrition.

Second year of cultivation:

From March throughout the year: constant weeding from asparagus weeds, weeding and when necessary irrigation.

Spring: a slight tamping of the rows is carried out.

June: The first asparagus shoots can be harvested two years after the asparagus planting, i.e. after the second spring. They are cut when their length exceeds 10 cm, leaving the thinnest ones. It is better not to exaggerate when harvesting because the asparagus is still young and therefore not in full production.

Autumn: you must cut the aerial part of the asparagus plants, then cover them with a layer of soil and over compost (or mature manure) preparing for the winter.

From the third year of cultivation:

From March throughout the year: usual cultivation operations (constant weeding, weed control, irrigation only in the case of dry soil).

Spring: asparagus shoots are harvested (until June).

Autumn: mowing and fertilising as usual.

Duration of cultivation: Asparagus is a plant grown over several years, it takes two years to start production, but then it can be kept for a dozen years. If there are no problems and it is kept well the cultivation can be kept even 15-20 years. The length is assessed based on productivity (after a dozen years the asparagus falls into production) and the possible spread of fungal diseases.

Asparagus growing and harvesting

Weed control and weed control. It is very important to keep the asparagus beds in the garden clean, avoiding the proliferation of weeds. This is the toughest job to do in the asparagus garden.

I am going to raise it. A small tamping is useful in the spring, especially if the cultivation is a "baulature".

Irrigation. The asparagus is constantly watered during the first two years, after rooting and development of the plants there is no need to water much, only to prevent the soil from drying out completely. In any case, it is important never to exaggerate with water doses (it is better to water frequently with little water).

Mulching. In addition to mulching with compost for the winter, you can also think about mulching in the spring to reduce manual weeding.

Green asparagus or white asparagus. White asparagus is obtained by covering the shoots with soil so that they remain softer and do not turn green. It is easier to grow classic green asparagus in the home garden, since covering the plants with soil to obtain white asparagus is a very demanding job.

Picking asparagus. The asparagus is harvested in a scalar way, you choose the shoots that are more than 12 cm high from the ground, with a small knife you cut a few centimetres below ground level. There is also a special tool for picking asparagus. The harvest generally lasts from April to June.

Main diseases of asparagus

Bad wine. Fungal disease that can attack asparagus. The fungus infects the base of the plant, then its subterranean parts and manifests itself first on roots and rhizomes, is then noticed at the base of the shoot. It can be recognized by a reddish veil to which the name of the disease is due. Like many fungal problems, even the bad wine in organic farming does not have many remedies other than removing infected plants. The risk of bad wine increases if asparagus is grown as a result of potatoes, turnips, celery, carrots, or alfalfa. It is also prevented by often pulling weeds, as the fungus attacks many of the weeds and from there it spreads easily to asparagus.

Fusarium. Fusarium is a fungus that can attack the root parts and rhizome of asparagus. It manifests itself with yellowing and withering of the plant, or with root rot. It is favoured by water stagnation, especially in case of humidity combined with mild temperatures. Consequently, in organic farming the advice is to prevent it by studying a draining soil, perhaps with raised flowerbeds.

Rust. Cryptogamic disease that affects the aerial parts of the plant, manifests itself in yellowish or reddish spots, can cause the drying up of the affected parts. Like Fusariosi, rust also affects asparagus in a hot, humid climate. If it is detected immediately, it can be contained by promptly removing the diseased parts.

Parasites affecting asparagus

Onion fly. Asparagus is part of the family of liliaceous plants, therefore relatives of onions. This type of fly is rejected by the carrot plants, but it is not a simple association, as the asparagusic is maintained for years. In this case, therefore, the bacillus thuringiensis can be used to eradicate this insect.

Aphids. Aphids can attack asparagus, causing malformations in the bearing of the plant. To defend organic cultivation, I recommend reading our aphid defence guide.

Aubergine

Eggplant is a rustic and easy to grow vegetable, resistant to drought and a lover of mild climates. This plant has a robust stem and is not prone to disease.

Climate and soil suitable for aubergines

Aubergines are a really disease-resistant crop, their main weak point is related to the climate, since the cold can stop the growth of the plant making it dwarf, while an excessive heat blocks the harvest: if the conditions are unfavourable, it is possible that there is a fall of the flowers, that is the abnormal and premature fall of the flowers with consequent loss of the fruits. However, do not worry, a few small precautions are enough to ensure the success of this vegetable and you can always protect the plant when the temperature is too high with shading nets, when it is too low with non-woven fabric.

Prepare the soil

Aubergines require soil rich in organic matter and nutrients, like other solanaceae such as tomato and pepper are quite demanding vegetables. The fact that the water does not stagnate is also important, particularly for organic farming: good soil tillage prevents most diseases. For these reasons, it is necessary to take care of the preparation of the soil, with a deep gouging, in order to make it loose and draining.

Fertilization at the plant

For this crop to be successful in the garden, it is important that the soil is fertile and well fertilized. Before transplanting or sowing, 3 to 8 kg of mature manure can be buried for every square metre cultivated. If you use manure or manure in pellets, i.e. a dried product, you can consider one tenth of these values. The right amount of manure depends on the characteristics of the soil and how much the garden has been exploited previously.

When fertilising, however, be careful that there must not be an excess of nitrogen, in order to avoid the fall of flowers, so even if the nutrient must not be lacking, care must be taken not to exaggerate with the fertiliser.

The right climate

Aubergines are quite delicate plants from the point of view of climate: they require excellent sun exposure and above all you must pay attention to temperatures. Below 9 degrees, the seedling is subject to climatic stress caused by the cold and risks remaining dwarf, so be careful especially at night. A temperature higher than 15 degrees will then be necessary for the flowers to grow (mutation of the flowers in fruit), while temperatures above 32 - 33 ° C cause the fall of the flowers.

Sowing the eggplant

This vegetable is usually sown in March in a protected seedbed, while the transplanting in the garden is usually done at the end of April or May, for what has been said above about the temperatures, it is necessary to place the seedlings in the field only when the temperatures are permanently above 9 degrees.

Direct sowing in the field is possible but not very convenient because you must wait too long to plant, and you lose part of the potential harvest. In the detailed explanation of how to sow aubergines, the whole operation is explained in detail.

Sixth of planting. In the open field the eggplant is placed at least 80 cm between the rows and 60 cm along the row, the plants develop enough and need space and light, so it is not convenient to put them too tight.

Pruning, support, and tamping

Braces. The arrangement of braces to support the plant is very useful, even if the stem of this vegetable lignifies well and is resistant. Some varieties of aubergine have fruits that weigh a lot and load the branches of a shrub with a limited stem, which could bend if it is not properly supported. Usually bamboo canes or special plastic poles are used to tie the stem as it grows.

Buckle. A light tamping operation, bringing a little soil back to the foot of the stem can be useful to strengthen it and therefore help the supports, setting the plant stable and well erected.

Pruning. As in the case of tomatoes, the axillary shoots should also be removed in order to optimise the production of the plant. This is not a real pruning; this operation is called in different ways according to the areas. You can read more about it in the article that talks about tomato pruning, being a similar operation.

How much and when to irrigate

The aubergine plant is drought-resistant because it has a root system that goes very deep. Irrigation should be progressive, ideally using a drip irrigation system.

However, the eggplant also loves sprinkling, which keeps the red spider away, unlike peppers and tomatoes where sprinkling favours downy mildew.

Pests and insects

Aphids. These tiny harmful insects are a common problem for most garden plants and do not even spare aubergines. The aphids go under the leaves, produce sticky honeydew that hinders photosynthesis and often spread virus to the plant. If intercepted immediately, they are counteracted by manual removal or Marseille soap, but if the infestation takes hold, various treatments can be used to eliminate them with biological insecticides. If there are ladybugs in the garden, they take care of them, as they are voracious predators of these lice. Learn more about how to defeat aphids.

Dorifora. As for the potato also the eggplant can be infested by this beetle, it is better to check it manually during the second half of May and remove eggs and larvae, the topic can be deepened reading the article on how to defend against Dorifora.

Red spider: it is kept away by watering the leaves and can be fought with sulphur, garlic, or Marseille soap. Even a manual control can stop the spread of these plant mites if the infestation is caught early. Read more about the defence against the red spider mite.

The premature fall of the flowers

We have already mentioned, talking about the suitable climate and the soil, the possible occurrence of the flower farmstead, which of course those who grow aubergines must try to avoid. It is not a real disease but a simple physiopathy due to an adverse climate or a nutritional imbalance.

The premature fall of aubergine flowers occurs mainly because the temperature is too high, so it happens in the very hot summer months: often production stops in July and starts again in September, as the eggplant requires temperatures between 15 and 30 degrees, while above 32-33 degrees the flowers fall before they bear fruit. This problem can also occur due to excess nitrogen in the soil or lack of water.

When harvesting the eggplant

The aubergines are harvested about ten days after the flowers have been attached, before the fruit becomes hard. It is a vegetable that produces from summer until November when the cold weather makes it difficult. The plant dies at the first frost spreading a smell like tobacco.

The ripe eggplant can be recognized by its shiny skin, the fruit then ages and is noticeable by the loss of shine, from here it takes on a yellowish-brown colour on the skin, which becomes hard and woody. It is therefore important not to wait too long for the harvest and choose the right moment.

Basil

Basil is also easy to grow on the balcony of the house because it does not require much care. The plant can also be grown at home during the winter period, taking care to place the pot in which it is grown on a windowsill where it can receive a good amount of light.

Basil prefers light and fertile soil.

Get a large pot, better if made of terracotta, and fill it with garden soil. Depending on the size of the pot you can decide how many plants to grow. For the needs of a family, 2 or 3 plants should be more than enough.

Basil is a typical summer plant and therefore the temperature has a great influence on the success of the cultivation.

Temperatures below 15 degrees strongly slow down the growth of this plant and below 10 degrees are often fatal.

If you grow basil at home, remember that the plant needs lots of light, but do not put it right on the windowsill just behind the glass.

The sun's radiation on the glass has a multiplying effect that could cause the leaves of the plant to burn.

Sowing basil

The basil is sown in February or March, in a hot box. Spread a few seeds on the ground and cover with a very thin layer of soil.

Keep the sowing soil moist by spraying water on the surface with a nebulizer.

As soon as the seedlings are sturdy enough you can transplant them directly into the soil, if you have a small plot for the garden or, if the pot is large enough, leave them in a pot if you want to grow basil on the balcony.

Spacer the basil plants about 30 centimetres apart and water them regularly, taking care, however, that the soil is not excessively damp.

The lighter our plants have, the more vigorous they will grow.

Basil transplanting

Transplanting a plant that is already a few centimetres high is the easiest way to guarantee a plant that will give us its fragrant leaves for a long time.

Also, in this case, however, you must pay much attention to temperature changes.

It often happens that in supermarkets you can find potted basil seedlings for sale; many people think about its long survival at home but as many are bitterly disappointed.

If you buy it at the supermarket take note of this: you will need to transplant it as soon as possible.

The basil seedlings from the supermarket are grown in a well heated environment and with added fertilizers that keep them beautiful and apparently healthy.

In fact, however, if you don't repot the plant immediately, placing it in a larger pot filled with fertile soil, the plant will already show signs of suffering after a week even if you continue to water it regularly.

The fact is that, once the fertilizers are removed, the water is not enough to keep alive a plant whose root system has saturated all the available space in the small pot in which it is sold and, once brought home, the soil becomes irreparably depleted and the plant perishes.

When you take the plant out of the pot, you will almost certainly notice that the roots wrapped around each other have formed a compact and inextricable bread of soil and some roots have probably come out of the holes at the bottom of the pot in search of new space.

This is a clear sign that the plant needs to be repotted, but the fact that we have such compact soil bread is, from another point of view, a facilitating factor.

Basil, in all its species, has a slender root system which risks tearing easily if the roots are discovered and this could cause a delay in subsequent rooting.

Immediately after taking it home, it is therefore a good idea to repot it and keep it indoors, in a well-lit and warm place, carefully away from draughts of cold air.

How to reinvigorate basil

When the basil plant loses vigour, it is not necessarily due to some disease.

Almost always the plant is indicating that it is suffering and that we must take action to restore optimal conditions for its vegetative cycle.

About the need for repotting to allow the root system to expand into the soil I have already written a few lines above.

If the pot were big enough it could be that the soil has exhausted the nutrients that the basil uses, and it is therefore good to add an organic fertilizer that restores the fertility of the soil.

If the leaves tilt downwards sadly, losing vigour, the plant will almost certainly tell us that there is a shortage of water and therefore a need for irrigation.

It is quite easy to ascertain this by simply feeling with one finger whether the soil is dry or damp.

If the problem is the lack of water, its administration has almost immediate effects and, by passing from the roots to the leaves, it restores the cellular tension of the plant which immediately regains vigour.

If the soil seems moist and the leaves are more prone to rotting than to dryness, then the opposite problem could occur, i.e. the plant has an excess of water.

Although basil, in the middle of its vegetative activity, needs regular watering, water stagnation is a serious problem for it as well as for many other plants.

When repotting it is always advisable to add some expanded clay to the bottom of the pot, so that the roots do not remain in direct contact with the water eventually present in the saucer.

Once the plant has reached a certain development, in order to invigorate it can be useful to chop the top, that is, to remove the leaves of the upper part to stimulate the growth of lateral shoots and prevent the plants from blooming too soon.

If you do not prune the tips the plant tends to stretch and become hard and woody.

By cutting the tips of the stems the plant will not blossom and will become even more productive by emitting new leaves.

Use basil when you need it by removing one leaf from one plant and then from the other to prevent the individual plants from weakening too much and try to take the leaves from the apical part where possible to keep the plant lower.

Basil varieties

Basil belongs to the Labiatae family whose botanical name is Ocymum.

Under this denomination are harvested about sixty species carrying a generic name to refer, etymologically, to the word "okimon", having the meaning of "perfume" or "olezzo".

The Ocymum Basilicum is, after all, the vegetable cultivation known in Italy and which has become an integral part of the Mediterranean cuisine.

Ocymum Basilicum, with several of its varieties and especially the 'minimum' variety (Ocymum Basilicum Minimum) is grown because of the intense and very pleasant aromatic scent that emanates from the leaves and from the whole plant in general.

Beans

Sowing period. The beans are sown between October and March, depending on the climate, the plant has an erect habit and reaches a height of one meter, producing 5-6 pods.

Sixth of planting. The beans are sown in rows 70 cm apart, on the row the seed is buried every 20 cm. If it does not emerge in time, the seeds risk being eaten by insects. The seeds are placed at a depth of 4-6 cm. To learn more, read the article that explains how to sow the beans in the garden.

Ideal climate and soil. The bean loves temperatures between 15 and 20 degrees, however not below 5 degrees and a pH of the soil between 5.5 and 6.5.

Growing

The bean is a simple vegetable to grow, the instructions on how to grow beans are practically the same for this vegetable. From the point of view of irrigation, the bean plants need water during flowering, so as soon as the first flowers sprout, you must ensure proper watering of the plants. The bean is afraid of prolonged drought but also of water stagnation, which causes rot and disease.

The cultivation after sowing, in addition to irrigation, includes weeding and weeding to control weeds and some hoeing to keep the soil soft. You can then make a tamping to protect the plant from the cold and stimulate the roots.

Adversity: diseases and insects

The bean is particularly afraid of aphids, not for nothing is the black bean aphid called "black bean aphid".

The weevil, on the other hand, is a beetle that can seriously damage the crop. From weevil and aphids, you can defend the beans by following the same guidelines as for beans.

Among the diseases the worst adversities are the charcoal of the bean, a fungus that in situations of prolonged humidity can make the roots of the plant rot.

Harvesting

The broad beans are harvested between May and June, before the seed becomes hard, and can also be eaten raw. If the seed is too ripe, the legume must be peeled before eating it. The right moment for harvesting occurs to the touch by feeling the seeds inside the pod.

The right moment for harvesting can occur by touching the seeds in the pod. The seed can be dried, taking the same precautions that are taken with the bean, in order to avoid the raids of the weevil.

Once harvested, the broad beans can be dried or stored frozen. When drying, be careful of the weevil (as with the bean). The dried broad beans can also be reduced to flour, which can then be used in the kitchen and in vegetable soups.

Broccoli

The climate and the soil. This cabbage is not particularly demanding in terms of the richness of the soil but is afraid of water stagnation. For this reason it is necessary to prepare the soil carefully by digging deep, if you are in a rainy area or with poorly draining soil it is better to raise the cultivation beds and think about a system of water drainage through channels. As a fertiliser, broccoli is content to follow a vegetable that is abundantly fertilised (e.g. courgette), taking advantage of its residual fertility.

Sowing. Cabbage broccoli is planted in early summer, usually in June and July. The best system is to sow it in honeycombed containers, in which the seedlings are developed and then transplanted into soil bread, about a month after germination. Producing the seedlings is extremely simple: just put some soil in the containers, place the seed a few millimetres deep and water it regularly. You can put 2-3 seeds in each container so that you can then choose the best seedling once germination has taken place. Cabbage seeds require a high enough temperature to be born but sowing it in summer does not require a heated seedbed.

Transplanting and distances. When the cabbage seedling is well developed, after about a month or more from the laying of the seed, it is time to transplant. The distance at which the seedlings are placed is at least half a metre from each other, in order to allow the broccoli to develop correctly, it is best to leave it even 60/70 cm.

The cultivation of broccoli

Weeding and weeding. Periodically the soil between the plants of the broccoli cabbage must be weeded, both to prevent the formation of a superficial crust and to defeat weeds. It can also be done with the help of a hoe and weedier, taking care not to damage the roots with the tool.

Irrigation. Broccoli needs to be wet, especially during the hot months, so that the soil never dries out completely. Rather than getting it very wet and rarely, it is better to proceed with frequent watering in moderate amounts.

Buckthorn. A tamping at the base of the plant is useful to make it more resistant and protect the collar.

Mulching. Mulching on cabbage crops can be useful: during the cold months it helps to keep the soil warm, during the summer months it preserves the soil humidity, and it also avoids the horticulturist a lot of work to pull weeds.

Harvest broccoli

Harvesting. Broccoli is harvested from the inflorescences, to be removed when they are formed and firm before the flowers open. Harvesting the inflorescence leaves the plant, which can throw more afterwards. The first lump is the central pome of the broccoli cabbage, then on the axillae the plant throws minor inflorescences, very good to eat, called broccoli. Generally, broccoli is harvested from October to December, in the southern regions you can also spend the winter.

Nutritive properties. Broccoli is renowned for its beneficial properties; the presence of many natural antioxidants makes it excellent for fighting cellular aging and useful in cancer prevention. These cabbages are also rich in mineral salts, fibre, and B vitamins.

Carrots

It is a vegetable that is not particularly difficult to cultivate but requires a soft, sandy soil, so it is not good in every vegetable garden.

The carrot seeds are a little slow to germinate, and it is better to plant them directly in the field, rather than putting them in the seedbed.

The right climate. Carrots require a climate that is not too hot, because the root hardens if the temperature is very high. In general, however, they adapt to all climates, whilst they are more demanding about the type of soil they encounter.

Soil. The soil is the real rock for those who want to grow carrots. This vegetable prefers a soft and loose soil, with water draining. Stony or compact soils are not good because the roots cannot develop properly. If the soil becomes hard the carrots remain small or grow deformed and twisted. To get a more suitable soil, you can mix sand with the soil of your vegetable garden where you plan to grow carrots. This must be done at least two months before sowing.

Soil preparation. Before planting the carrots, you must work the soil to make it very loose, then you need to make a deep digging (about 40 cm deep), placing compost or other organic fertilizer.

Fertilization. To fertilise carrot plants, compost is better than manure: the higher nitrogen content in manure risks favouring the development of leaves at the expense of the root. Whatever fertilisation is chosen, however, attention must be paid not to exaggerate with nitrogen: since the root is obviously the part of the vegetable that is consumed and that is interested in harvesting, it would make no sense to give a fertiliser dedicated to the leaves.

When and how to sow carrots in the garden

No transplants. Being a taproot plant, carrots cannot be sown in a seedbed: this vegetable must be planted directly in the ground. Carrots do not tolerate a possible passage from the pots to the garden: if you sow in trays you will get deformed roots.

Sowing period. This vegetable is generally sown in spring, between March and June. In the family garden it can be sown several times in order to have a scalar production. There are early varieties that can be sown in February and late varieties that can be sown until October, if you help yourself with a tunnel to preserve the vegetable from frost you can have carrots practically all year round.

Sixth of planting. You can sow in rows, but it is preferable to do it in rows, avoiding close distances, which create too much competition between the roots. The distance between rows should be 25 cm, while along the row at least 5 cm (the optimal distance between plants is 8 cm). The seed must be buried at a depth of one centimetre.

How to sow. The carrot seed is very small, you can facilitate sowing by mixing a little sand with the seeds or by making strips of wet newsprint with a natural glue to be buried. There are also strips of ready-to-spread or candied seeds on the market, which are larger because of the coating. In any case it is necessary to check that the sugared or ribbon is in natural substances, to ensure that the biological method is respected.

Slow germination. The carrot seed germinates at temperatures between 12 and 20 degrees, the carrot has a particularly slow germination, it can take up to 40 days to emerge. So, do not be frightened if you do not see the young seedlings appear immediately: a lot of patience is needed. A cover with non-woven fabric helps to warm up and can accelerate germination.

Seed bath. Soaking the seeds in warm water or chamomile tea a few hours before sowing can also help to accelerate germination.

How to grow carrots

Weed control. Since the germination of carrot seeds is slow, competition from garden weeds with frequent weeding by hand near the seeds and with the hoe in the spaces between the rows should be avoided. With carrots you can also use the pyro weeding technique.

Thinning the seedlings. If the plants are too thick it is necessary to thin out the seedlings, eliminating the more stunted ones and leaving at most one seedling every 5 centimetres. The operation must be done when the carrot emits the fourth leaf and the area part is at a height of 3-4 centimetres.

Hoeing and hoeing. A slight tamping may be necessary if the roots emerge from the ground, in order to prevent light from turning the carrot collar green. When the top of the root turns green it is not good to eat, this does not mean having to discard the whole carrot, just cut the greenish piece. Apart from the tamping, moving the soil between the rows with the hoe is a very useful operation to keep the soil around the root soft, making it often helps to produce beautiful carrots of good size.

Mulching. If the vegetable garden is exposed to the wind or in any case tends to create a crust on the soil, it is best to protect the cultivation with mulching, which prevents the soil from drying out and therefore hardening. This obviously replaces the tamping and hoeing operations.

Irrigation. Carrots do not need constant humidity, just irrigate when the soil becomes dry, watering should never create stagnation, which causes diseases to the plant.

Subsidization. Carrots and onions take advantage of each other's association, in fact, one drives away the parasites of the other (the carrot drives away the onion fly and the leek worm, vice versa the onion drives away the carrot fly). You can also replace the onion with leek, garlic, or shallot. A good neighbourhood in the synergistic garden is also that between radish and carrot.

Succession and turnover. It is not advisable to repeat the carrot to itself, the carrot is well followed by solanaceous plants such as tomato or potato, but also legumes, for example peas, or garlic and leek. It is best to avoid carrots with cabbage, asparagus, onion, all Chenopodiaceae and other umbrella plants (such as fennel and celery).

Insects and pests of this crop

Underground worms. Other enemies of this root vegetable are subterranean pests: nematodes produce lumps on the root, while the underwires or Elaterides pierce it.

Carrot Fly: This fly lays its eggs in the aerial part of the carrot; its larvae then begin to eat the plant when it hatches. This fly fortunately cannot stand the smell of Liliaceae (leek, shallot, garlic, and onion). Hence the onion technique, from which the onion also benefits because the carrot in turn is unwelcome to the onion fly. A completely natural method to keep the parasite away.

Aphids. The attack of aphids is particularly difficult to detect because of the shape of the leaves: you need a lens to detect them and the symptom of an attack may be the lack of growth of the leaf part. Carrot aphids can be fought with pyrethrum, a biological insecticide to be used in extreme cases, more natural and less toxic remedies are garlic decoction or nettle macerate.

When to pick carrots

Carrots have a cultivation cycle of 75 - 130 days depending on the variety sown, so they are generally harvested two months after sowing. Usually the root is harvested when its diameter exceeds one centimetre and is under two centimetres. If you leave too much in the soil, the heart, which is the central part tending to white, hardens in the old carrot and becomes woody and therefore unpleasant to eat.

The carrots are harvested by eradicating the root, it is advisable to soften the soil the days before, watering often.

To keep the carrots harvested it is necessary to let them dry in a ventilated and not very humid environment, after which this vegetable keeps well if kept cool.

In the family garden you can sow the carrots staggered to have a scalar harvest that allows the horticulturist to bring fresh carrots to the table for a good part of the year. The protected cultivation in tunnels extends the period of possible cultivation to a good part of the winter months.

Celery

The cultivation of this vegetable does not require any special care other than bleaching to obtain softer stems to eat.

Climate. Celery loves temperate climates that see the thermometer around 20 degrees and fears frost, which can lead to early flowering. It prefers the sun but also tolerates growing in half-light.

Soil. Ideal for celery is a soil rich in organic substances, which is constantly humid although without stagnation. The celery flowerbed must be worked in depth to obtain a draining and soft soil. It can be fertilised with compost or mature manure, to be distributed in moderation.

Sowing celery

Sow. Celery is always transplanted in the garden, because its initial growth phase is very slow and therefore if sown directly in the garden it would occupy the space of the flowerbed for too long. Transplanting must take place when the seedling has grown over 4-5 cm, a size that celery reaches two months after germination. A double transplant is often used: putting it first in the seedbed and then in the pot, at the tick of the first real leaf (the cotyledons of celery are very small). From the jar it will then finally reach its destination in the garden.

Sowing period. The sowing in a jar takes place at the end of winter, between February and March, given the time of growth of the seedling is not worth going further. Transplanting can be done from May until the end of July.

Sixth of planting. The distance to keep growing celery in the garden is 35 x 35 centimetres, with this space the plants can develop well.

Cultivation technique and useful tips

Irrigation. Celery loves water very much, it is a plant of marshy origin and does not produce without water supply, for this reason it must be irrigated every 2 or 3 days. For those who grow many plants, it is better to think about making a drip plant, especially if the field is in hot and arid climate zones.

Mulching. Since celery loves heat and water, it can make very good use of mulching, which is a highly recommended cultivation technique in this crop. Soil cover helps to keep the soil moist, which is very important.

Mulching. If you decide not to mulch, it is necessary to oxygenate the soil by moving it with periodic hoeing, both to make it soft and to control weeds. The celery plant grows slowly and can be subject to weed competition.

Whitening. To make the celery softer the technique of bleaching is used, obtained with two sheets of polythene placed vertically and tied to the two sides of the plant. Tamping is used less because it requires a lot of space between rows. After 15 days of bleaching the green celery takes on a pale colour tending to white and becomes very tender, otherwise it remains hard and filamentous. Bleaching also provides an extension of the harvesting period because it protects the plant from frost and can last until Christmas.

Harvesting celery

Celery is harvested between September and October, you must choose the right time because otherwise it turns yellow and dry, becoming hard. The celery plant does not grow in seed in the year because it would be biennial, growing it annually you never see it flowering. It is harvested by cutting the plant at the collar, after cutting it would theoretically grow a new stem. As the plant is now old, it has a lower productivity and quality of the vegetables, therefore, usually, it avoids harvesting the shoots.

Cucumber

Cucumber is an interesting vegetable, simple enough to grow with natural methods, only requires frequent watering, topping and some other care that we will learn shortly.

Its varieties can be distinguished in long cucumbers and gherkins, the latter are generally pricklier. This vegetable is suitable for fresh consumption, salad cucumbers, but also to be preserved pickled, gherkins to be put in pots. We can therefore think of it to obtain a harvest to be brought to the table immediately or to be preserved for the winter, this makes it certainly a plant recommended for the home garden.

Indicated climate. The cucumber is a plant that wants warm, therefore it requires high temperatures, while it fears frost. For this reason, it is a typical summer vegetable.

Soil. This cucurbitaceous plant adapts quite well to different soils; however, it needs a constantly humid soil. The ideal soil is draining, well exposed to the sun, rich in nutrients and tending to acid.

Cultivation and fertilization for cucumber

Before planting the cucumber plant it is very important to work the soil correctly, in order to prepare it in the best possible way and also to carry out a correct background fertilization, which will support the crop by providing all the substances useful for its survival.

A good spading is particularly useful to guarantee a draining soil, as well as to prepare the right habitat for the roots of the plant. If we want to transplant already formed seedlings, it is essential that the root system immediately finds a soft soil in which to penetrate. To the work of spade follows the hoe, in the most superficial part and then the rake to level the whole.

When hoeing, we can also take advantage of it to incorporate organic matter as a soil conditioner and fertilizer. Fertilization is fundamental to have a good harvest. As far as nutrients are concerned, cucumbers are particularly fond of potassium: if there is no nutrient, the fruit swells at the tip, while if there is no nitrogen, there is a deformation to the contrary. Therefore, be careful not to miss these elements. The base is always a complete organic soil improver (compost or mature manure), which we can integrate with other substances allowed in bio, such as rock flour, algae, wood ash. Ash for its potassium content is an excellent idea, but without exaggeration because it is basic.

Cucumber sowing and transplanting

After having spat and fertilized, it is time to plant these plants in our garden. We can choose to sow directly in the field or in the seedbed, but also to buy the plants ready to transplant in the nursery. The important thing is to do it in the right period let us not forget that too low temperatures (below 15 degrees) can seriously damage the plant.

Sixth of planting. Whether you plant the seed or the seedling, it is also important to respect a large planting season: like other cucurbits, cucumbers are also a rather bulky species. The right size depends on which variety you decide to plant, on average the rows should be drawn 100 cm apart, with 50 cm between each plant along the row. In case of direct sowing we can also decide to put the cucumbers at 20 cm, and then thin out.

Sowing: how to do it, the period, and the moon

Sowing period. Cucumbers are planted in a protected crop between February and April, so that they stay in the seedbed until the temperature stabilises. From April to June you can plant the cucumber directly in the garden, the important thing is to take care of the minimum temperatures, even at night.

Cucumber sowing and moon phases. Many farmers, even professionals, rely on the moon phases to determine the sowing period. Despite my personal scepticism, I would like to tell you about the tradition: the cucumber is a fruit vegetable and should therefore be planted in a crescent moon, which would favour the aerial part of the plant, the production of flowers and fruits.

The cucumber plant should only be planted when it is certain that no more night frosts will occur, as it is a crop that is particularly sensitive to cold. If we have grown the seedling ourselves, then we should also wait until it is sufficiently developed, making sure that it has emitted the first two real leaves (the first two leaves are called "cotyledons"). Transplanting is a very simple job; we can learn more about how to do it by reading the article dedicated to how to transplant a vegetable garden seedling correctly.

Cultivation of cucumbers

After planting let us see what we need to do to get a good cucumber harvest. The organic cultivation of this horticultural species is not particularly complicated, but some precautions are necessary to have productive and healthy plants.

Productivity and flower setting

If we want to harvest cucumbers, it is essential to first take care of the pollination aspect. There are self-pollinating cucumber varieties (parthenocarpy), others that produce only female flowers to which, for pollination to take place, other pollen varieties must be associated. When choosing the seed or seedling, you should inform yourself.

During growth, the cucumber normally produces a leaf and a flower, in the gherkins the flowers can be presented in clusters: if they enclose all the flowers the production will be very high. Bees and other pollinators, which are the natural ones responsible for fertilising the female flowers, should therefore be treated well. First, you must avoid the use of pesticides, it may be useful to plant some plants with flowers they like, such as marigold or borage. In case of emergency you can still pollinate the flowers manually, with a small brush.

Vertical cultivation

Although it depends on the variety, in most cases it is better to grow cucumbers vertically, as creepers. The advantage is primarily in the smaller footprint in square meters, but not only.

Cultivating with supports that hold the plant in height greatly favours pollination and therefore production. In addition, vertical cultivation saves weeding work and makes it easier to harvest the fruit.

For this reason, it is necessary to set up braces, you can use poles, including pulling wires, sticks or nets. Cucumber supports must reach a height of 150 cm. Sometimes the perimeter fences of vegetable gardens or gardens are used to make you climb our climbing cucumber.

Weeding, mulching, and irrigation

Like all cucurbits, mulching is a popular practice for cucumber, and for the horticulturist who avoids a lot of effort in weeding. As the covering reduces perspiration and keeps the soil moist, it saves water and therefore less irrigation.

If you do not mulch, remember to weed periodically, hoeing the flowerbed soil around the cucumbers. Being a climbing plant held vertically is a job that you only need to do sporadically, much less demanding than other lower vegetable crops.

In terms of irrigation, cucumbers love plenty of water, but not stagnation. It is therefore necessary to irrigate often, if possible, keeping the soil constantly moist (40-45% moisture content). The aridity, even for a short period, besides endangering the health of the plant, makes the fruit bitter or causes it to empty inside.

How to prune the cucumber: the topping

Cucumber is a quite exuberant plant in its development, that is why on most of its varieties it is useful to prune it in order to direct its energies towards a better productivity.

Usually the advice is to prune the cucumber plants by cutting the main stem above the fifth leaf. This topping stimulates the horizontal branches and speeds up the plant's entry into production.

Harmful insects

Among the parasites, the aphids are generally the worst enemy of the cucumber, the species aphis gossypii or cucurbitaceous aphid. In the organic vegetable garden the advice is to try to keep them away by using repellent vegetable macerates (garlic, chilli, fern, rhubarb,) and resort to insecticide treatments only in extreme cases and using only environmentally friendly products (potassium soft soap, Neem oil, nettle macerate). For cucumber aphids, pruning can also be used as a means of stopping an infestation, eliminating the affected parts.

Cucumber harvesting

Harvested. For the cucumber as for the zucchini, the rule applies that by harvesting the plant is encouraged to continue to produce, while leaving fruit to age on the plant is lost a lot, also decreasing its future productivity.

Degree of ripeness. The cucumber is in fact eaten unripe, so even when it is very small it is very good to pick. We can decide to harvest the cucumber to taste, choosing whether to do so when it is still small or let it swell, a good average size for many varieties is to reach a length of 20 cm. However, it is important to pick the fruit before it turns yellowish, losing its thorns. These are the symptoms of cucumber aging, if you see them you have already passed the best time to pick your vegetables.

Period. The cucumbers are usually picked from the beginning of summer and then proceed for about three months, the plant suffering the first cold weather stops bearing fruit in autumn.

How to make cucumber seeds

If every year we grow cucumbers in our organic vegetable garden we can decide to preserve the cucumber seeds, so that we have them available to sow the following year and do not have to buy seeds. If we want to preserve the variety, we need to grow only one type of cucumber and make sure that there are no plants of other varieties in the surroundings, otherwise there will easily be crossbreeds. Alternatively, we can proceed with manual pollination. To make cucumber seeds it is also important to start from non-hybrid varieties (see more about what F1 hybrids are).

At this point it is easy to save the seeds: you have to leave one or more fruits on the plant until they are completely ripe, from here you have to extract the seeds and then clean them from the pulp and let them dry. Be careful not to try to take seeds from a green consumer cucumber: it is still unripe, and they are not ready.

Storage and use

After the harvest, the cucumber is kept in the refrigerator for about ten days. It is a vegetable very rich in water and for this reason it is pleasant in summer, it is basically eaten only raw, very good in salad.

A piece of advice to prepare it, making the most of it: after having cut it into slices and sprinkled with salt, leave it to rest for a few minutes: it will lose some water, tasteless... It becomes much tastier.

We can then decide to prepare the famous pickled gherkins. It is undoubtedly advisable to pick the cucumbers early, to have small fruits. Another excellent way to preserve them is salt, making a jar of brine. You can read the instructions on how to prepare the pickled gherkins in brine at best.

From the point of view of nutritional properties and benefits of course first stands out for the water content, accompanied by vitamin C, mineral salts, and amino acids. It is a very healthy vegetable that helps the body to withstand the summer heat. It can also be used in cosmetics for skin care, as a softener and after sun.

Fennel

The fennel plant forms a white lump at the base, which is the grower's vegetable of interest. There is also a wild variety, the fennel, which is cultivated as aromatic because of its fragrant leaves.

Ideal climate for cultivation. What is essential to know about the climate is that the fennel fears temperatures below 7 degrees and above 30. This umbellifer is sensitive to daylight hours, needs 12 hours of light and grows in seed if they increase, for this reason it should be sown in March or between June and July and can also be counted among the winter vegetables. Fennel is afraid of frost and for this reason it must be harvested before the winter frosts.

Soil suitable for fennel. The lump of fennel develops at ground level and for this reason, in order to cultivate it successfully, it is very important to take care of the soil and its processing. This horticultural plant does not tolerate stagnation, which is why you need a well tilled and draining soil, which allows a good prevention of cryptogamic diseases.

Fertilization. As far as fertilization is concerned, it prefers a fertile soil, better if fertilized beforehand (manure or compost are fine), without excesses. A little nitrogen can then be added during cultivation to encourage the growth of the lump.

Sowing fennel

Sowing fennel is not difficult, you can do it both directly in the field and in the seedbed, the work can be deepened by reading the article on how to sow fennel.

Sowing period: you can sow both in March, to harvest in June, and in June July, for autumn harvest. Those who want to follow the lunar phase will have to do it during the waning moon.

The sixth planting must be 30 cm between one plant and the other, along rows placed at 50/70 cm. The seed must be buried at a depth of about 1.5 cm. If you sow directly in the ground, it is better to sow close enough and then thin out by thinning out the seedlings until you leave them at the right distance.

The sixth planting determines the shape of the vegetable: if it is planted thickly it develops elongated and flattened, if it has space, we will have rounder fennel. The shape and size then depend on various other factors such as variety, type of soil, tamping.

How to grow fennel in the garden

Cultivating fennel is not difficult, but getting good-sized vegetables requires a lot of care, especially if the soil is not more than favourable.

Transplanting and weed control. Since this horticultural plant fears competition from weeds, it is often used to sow fennel in seedbeds and transplant them, in this way the already formed seedling is planted in the garden, able to compete with weeds. In any case, the fennel needs frequent weeding both to keep the soil soft and to avoid weeds.

Irrigation. Fennel needs a soil that is always wet, even without stagnation. For this reason, it is necessary to water often, especially in the vegetable gardens located in very hot areas. A lack of water puts the plant under stress, which can go into pre-flowering and ruin the harvest.

Protection from the cold. Since fennel fears frost, it must be harvested before temperatures drop below freezing, or to get this vegetable in winter by extending the harvest period you can protect it using tunnels or non-woven fabric. If the temperature drops gradually, the fennel adapts a little and loses water, while a change in climate quickly ruins it.

Bleaching and tamping

Bleaching fennel is an important part of cultivation, as if done well it improves both the quality and size of the vegetable. A very common mistake among fennel growers is to tamp down the formed lump. The lump of fennel, which is then the vegetable, should not be tamped: it consists of leaves and a tamping would only facilitate attacks by insects and pests. The tamping operations are very useful for bleaching but must be carried out earlier: you can proceed with a single tamping 15 days before harvesting or with three or four tamping operations to be carried out while the lumps become larger.

Harvest and culinary use

Harvesting. Fennel is harvested about 80-120 days after sowing, the length of the cultivation cycle depends on the variety. The lump is always edible, obviously choosing the right time for harvesting maximizes the size and quality: if you take too cold the vegetables remain small, waiting too long there is a risk that they harden, especially in the outer layers, and therefore become unpleasant, especially if eaten raw.

Use. Fennel is a versatile vegetable in the kitchen: raw vegetables have a fresh and crunchy taste, they are perfect in summer salads, cooked they become a more classic side dish, they can be boiled or baked, they are delicious especially the fennel au gratin.

Lettuce

Lettuce loves quite cool temperatures and for this reason it is an ideal vegetable to grow in autumn and spring. It grows well in a protected crop and for this reason it can be harvested practically all year round if scalar sowing is carried out and it is also grown in tunnels. It is a plant that is not very demanding in terms of space and substances in the soil, which can also be grown in pots on the balcony.

Climate. All varieties of lettuce, both head and cut lettuce, need cool temperatures: they germinate ideally between 10 and 18 degrees. When temperatures rise above 22 degrees the seeds no longer germinate, which is why they are optimal vegetables for growing in spring and autumn and suffer during the summer months.

Soil. Lettuce is undemanding, being better able to choose a loose, fertile, and draining soil, but there are no particular demands in terms of soil.

How to sow lettuce

Sowing head lettuces. The head varieties can be sown directly in the field or in the seedbed. If you want to plant the seeds directly in the vegetable garden, they are usually placed in small pots, while in protected cultivation they are germinated in jars, which can also be left initially in a cool place to protect them from the summer heat, for example in the cellar, or heated during the winter months. Once the first small leaves have grown, the salad plants require light. The sowing period is very long: December/January if kept under shelter, February/March in seedbed or protected crop and then in open field from April until June. Distances depend on the variety of lettuce; the best-known species form large tufts and require distances of at least 35 cm between plants. The seeds are placed in posts with 2-3 seeds each, at a depth of one centimetre.

Sow cutting lettuces. They are usually sown directly in the field, in rows. The row has the advantage of an easier cleaning from weeds, moreover you avoid too close distances which generate fungal diseases. In spring and early autumn, the seeds are planted in the garden, but if you plant under a tunnel or tarpaulin, you can also start in February and continue until the end of November.

Sow lettuce in summer. Lettuce germinates at temperatures below 22 degrees Celsius, if you want to sow in the warm months you need to keep the soil cool, for example you can cover the flowerbeds with a burlap sack that needs to be wet often, in this way evaporation cools and allows the salad to develop in spite of the high outside temperatures.

Lettuce growing

Cultivating the salad is very simple, once sown you just need to be careful to give the right amount of water and keep weeds and insects under control, especially larvae and snails. If the climate becomes adverse or the water lacks, it can happen that the plant decides to seed in advance, and emits the floral scape, ruining the harvest.

Transplant the salad. If you sow the lettuce in a jar at the time of transplanting, remember to keep a finger of bread out of the ground and not to flush the soil. This will allow the head that develops laterally to stay elevated, avoiding rotting due to the crushing of leaves on the ground.

Mulching. A very useful technique to save weeding work is to use mulching to grow lettuce. You can mulch it with straw or organic jute cloth.

Irrigation. The wide leaves of the salad are very breathable and for this reason frequent irrigation is recommended. The moments of greatest need for water are immediately after transplanting and when the head forms. Evening watering in the evening prevents many fungal diseases such as "bremia", you should avoid wetting the leaves and watering during times of great heat.

Lettuces in winter. The lettuce sown in winter stops its growth with frost, if the leaves are few and still small the plant can resist the winter and start again at the first warmth to have the salad ready in spring. You can protect the lettuce with non-woven fabric or grow it in a tunnel, for more information see the article on how to grow winter salads. Head lettuces are less resistant to cold than cut lettuce varieties.

Harvesting and use. The lettuce is harvested before it grows to seed, usually within 80-100 days of cultivation, including 2-3 weeks in seedbeds. The canasta is a little longer and grows to seed in 4 months, but it gets a lot of damage on the outer leaves, the lollo is the fastest to develop. If you want to slow down the ascent to seed, a watering of very cold water causes a shock to the plant and stops it for a few days. When harvesting head lettuces, you usually cut the whole head. However, you can opt for the milking method.

Cutting varieties, on the other hand, allow more harvests each year: you cut the salad leaves, then wait for them to grow again for a second harvest. There are three cuts per variety such as lollo and snake. The lettuce (green or red) forms lumps to be harvested in spring.

Insects and parasites

Ferretti. In the earth, Elaterides can ruin the lettuce seedlings, to get rid of them you can attract them with pieces of potato and then eliminate them manually.

Caterpillars. The larvae of "oziorrinco" and "maggiolino" are caterpillars that come out at night to eat the plant, especially at the collar. Bacillus thuringensis, a non-toxic and natural method, can be used against them.

Aphids. Aphids are small insects that are very difficult to eliminate because the lettuce head offers many ravines in which these lice can nest. Pyrethrum is an insecticide that could kill them but acts by contact and although natural it has a slight toxicity, so it is better to avoid it. If the infestation is not very advanced, it is enough to wash away the aphids, if some specimen remains and is eaten, it will be just a few more proteins.

Snails. Other enemies of the salad are slugs and snails, these gastropods literally eat lettuce leaves. Snail attacks are easy to identify and stop with traps made with jars filled with beer or other bait.

Melon

Climate. The melon is a plant typical of hot climates, so the seed begins to germinate above 24 degrees and loves a climate around 30 degrees, fears frost and just that the temperature drops below 14 degrees to cause vegetative stasis and inhibit growth.

Soil. We are talking about a plant belonging to the cucurbitaceous family which requires a soil very rich in nutrients, which is possibly not very acidic, humid but which absolutely does not have water stagnations. The melon is a potassophilous plant (potassium is used to increase the quantity of sugars) and, therefore, the soil should be enriched using compost or ash.

Sowing in jars and transplanting. In seedbeds, melons can be sown between March and April, transplanting at the end of April when temperatures are permanently temperate and go towards warm and sunny days.

It sows directly in the open field. The melon seeds can be planted directly in the seedbed, making a small hole where 3-4 seeds are placed, it will then thin out leaving only the two best seedlings. You sow between mid-April and May.

Sixth of planting. The melon is sown at a maximum of one plant per square meter, we recommend one meter between the plants, arranged in rows 100-150 cm apart.

The cultivation of the melon step by step

Pest control. The melon requires frequent weeding if you want to avoid it you can think about mulching.

Mulching. Excellent practice in growing melons, especially because it warms the soil and defends the fruit from the Elaterides that could pierce them.

Irrigation. The melons should be wetted a little during the initial growth, then gradually increase because the large leaves perspire a lot and the melon grows in the warmer seasons. When the fruits turn from green to yellow or white/grey, the water supply is reduced to keep the fruits sweeter.

Pruning. The melon blooms on its secondary branches, so it is good practice to prune the plant after its fifth leaf, this way it emits axillary branches and anticipates flowering.

Products to increase sugar. There are specific products to spray the leaves of melon and make the fruit more sugary, they are not allowed in organic farming and we strongly advise against them if as we believe in the goodness of fruit and vegetables that are healthy and natural.

Fruit care. The fruit should be kept isolated from the ground, to prevent it from rotting or being attacked by pests such as Elaterides or ferrets, so it is best to place it on a wooden board. A small pile of straw or mulch may also be enough.

Vertical cultivation. The fruit supports itself until it ripens, so you can also grow melons vertically, using a wire mesh. In this case better hybrid varieties such as long life or middle long life, have hard flesh, increase sugar gradually and do not detach easily from the plant.

Sub associations and rotations. The melon looks good next to salads and onions, as a crop rotation better to wait 4 years before growing it again in the same place and take into account not to grow it where there had been other cucurbits.

Insects and diseases to defend melons from

There are several fungal diseases that can attack the melon plant, the worst are Pitium and Verticillium:

- Verticilium: brings first tracheomicosi of the plant and then death.
- Pitium: acts only at low temperatures and humidity, so in most cases it does not bother, it attacks the plant to the collar and causes it to rot.
- Viruses (cucumber mosaic). It slows down the growth of both the plant and the fruit or causes deformation. It is important to prevent the aphids from spreading to the cucumber mosaic.
- Aphids. Frequent inspections are needed to protect plants from attacks by these plant lice, protection such as non-woven fabric on young plants or anti-aphid nets can be used. However, these protections must be removed as

soon as the flowers appear so that the insects can pollinate them. The melon lives during the warm months, when the aphids then stay away from the plants, so only the first period is critical for the aphids.

When harvesting this fruit

Melon cultivation takes about 120/160 days between sowing and harvesting. When ripe, the fruit of the melon detaches itself, a small twist is enough to attach the fruit to the plant. The colour of the skin is useful to understand if the melon is ready for harvesting. The sugars of the melon are concentrated in the last week of growth, so be careful to pick it ripe, otherwise it remains bland. The lack of potassium in the soil also causes tasteless melons. The advice is to wait a few hours to eat it, better still at least one day. A melon kept in the fridge will keep for 10 days.

To learn more about harvesting this fruit I recommend reading the post dedicated to when to pick the melon.

There are the so-called winter melons, with pale flesh and green or yellow skin, in this case it is more difficult to understand the right time when the fruit is ripe.

Usually the summer melon takes 60 days to ripen from the flower setting, while the winter melon is slower (80-100 days).

A little known and interesting news ... At the end of the harvest on the plants of melons remain some fruit that will not have time for proper ripening, not wasted: you can put pickles and are delicious, sweeter than cucumbers.

Mint

Mint is a plant of very easy cultivation and it will be easy to taste its taste for many years, once planted.

Mentha spicata is the species that is most cultivated, although many prefer the species with rounded leaves, Mentha rotundifolia, which is also called by other different names: mint, mintspru, mint. This second variety is grown in the same way but is less susceptible to rust.

Mint is a perennial plant that is cultivated mainly for its refreshing and aromatic virtues; you can prepare mint tea or use it in many cocktails.

Mint is a plant that needs full sun or light shade and loves rich and naturally moist soils.

Planting takes place in autumn or spring. You can buy the seedlings in the nursery or simply get some roots as a gift from a neighbour or relative who should not refuse them. In fact, mint is a very intrusive plant and spreads through rhizomatous roots in an extremely easy way. If you don't want the plant to take possession of all the soil, which you may have dedicated to aromatic plants, you need to dig a groove 30 or 40 centimetres deep around the space dedicated to it or bury wooden planks all around the perimeter.

In a short time, your mint plant will grow luxuriant to a height of 30-45 centimetres.

Once the plant has become strong enough you can peel off the leaves for our needs. If you want to have a second harvest in the autumn, you need to cut the plant in June.

As has already been written, mint multiplication takes place through the roots, so it is enough to divide the rhizomes into two or more parts and replant them to obtain individual plants.

Mint can also be enjoyed out of season if we have the care to dry or freeze its leaves.

Onion

Climate. This liliaceous plant resists the cold very well, so much so that it can be planted in autumn and spend the winter in the field. What she does not like are the climatic excursions that are too strong. It prefers sunny areas.

Soil preparation. The most suitable soils for the onion plant are ventilated and not very compact, with a pH between 6 and 7, while it finds difficulties in clayey and asphyxiated soil. It fears above all water stagnation, a source of rot and disease. Since the onions require loose soil, it is essential to carry out a good tillage of the soil, to be done months before sowing. Deep tillage is not essential if the soil is already draining, but it is important that the soil does not remain compact.

Fertilization

The onion is a plant with low nutrient requirements and does not like recently fertilised soils and excess nutrients. For this reason, it is better to avoid specific fertilization before planting, better to feed the soil a few months before sowing and without exaggerating. An excellent system in a mixed vegetable garden is to put the onion inside a crop rotation following a vegetable demanding in terms of substance, such as pumpkin or zucchini, in this way our lilliacee will be satisfied with the residual fertility left by the predecessor vegetable.

How and when to sow onions

Planting onions is a very simple operation, which can be done at different times of the year, depending on the variety of onion chosen, and also in different ways, starting from the seed, the bulb or putting the seedling.

There are three ways to plant onions in the vegetable garden: the onions can be sown by planting the seed directly in the vegetable garden, always sowing from seed into seedbeds and then transplanting the seedlings or planting the bulbs in the soil. The latter is not a real sowing, as there is no seed involved. If you sow in the seedbed, the onions are transplanted after about 1 month and a half or two, when the seedlings are 15 cm high.

The ideal is to start from the seeds, putting them directly into the soil and avoiding transplanting, which the onion plant does not particularly like. The bulb is a very convenient method and is generally cheaper than buying seedlings in a nursery. It can be a good idea for those who do not have time or desire to follow a seedling from the beginning.

Sixth of planting

The onions are grown in rows 25-30 cm apart, leaving about 20 cm between each plant. This measure is very indicative and is referred to the classic bulb onions: if we decide to grow spring onions, which are harvested for the leaves, we can reduce the measure to halve it. The planting size also varies depending on the variety, for example the borettane onions that remain small area sown very close together.

Keeping a regular space between the rows is important to be able to weed with a hoe or a weeder, which is also useful for aerating the soil, especially if the soil tends to compact. So, when sowing and transplanting, always remember to pull a line or make parallel and straight furrows.

Variety and sowing period

Onions have different varieties with different growing periods. Usually red onions are early, white semi-early and late golden onions, although several exceptions to these rules have been created with selection. The sowing periods are different and there are winter varieties and spring varieties, it is important not to make mistakes because there is a risk that the plant will bloom, ruining the harvest. Those who want to go deeper into the subject can read the article on onion sowing, which explains better period, distances, and suitable moon phase. In any case, always remember to buy a seed suitable for our climate and the period in which we want to sow.

Winter onions. There are varieties of onions, especially used for fresh consumption, which are sown in September and transplanted in November, after winter they develop the bulb that can be harvested in April or May. If you choose to plant winter onion bulbs you can do so in November. Generally winter sowing is done for golden onions or white onions.

Summer onions. Summer varieties are sown at the end of winter (in February in the seedbed, between March and April they are transplanted in the garden), in February or March to plant the bulbs. They are ready in summer and generally keep longer. Summer onions can be of any colour: white, golden or red.

Spring onions. Spring onions are always botanically onions, grown for the leaves rather than the bulb. Just like the bulb onions, they can be grown from autumn to spring (sowing in October or November) or from spring to summer (sowing between March and April).

Weed control. Weeding is important to protect the onions from weeds, as onion plants do not cover much of the surrounding soil and can therefore struggle to compete with spontaneous vegetation. Good weed control ensures that our crop has enough space and nutrients to grow well and swell the bulb.

Weed control. Oxygenating the soil and keeping it loose is very important, my advice is to use the hoe at least 3-4 times when growing onions to break the crust of the soil but be careful not to damage the roots. If you have a clayey soil you should pass it even more often.

Mulching. If you do not have time to weed the soil regularly and want a vegetable garden that requires as little time as possible, you can opt for mulching the soil with a cloth or straw. Onions, because of their planting pattern, are particularly suitable for the use of straw, a natural and biodegradable material at no cost. Mulching also saves on irrigation, since the soil cover helps to retain moisture.

Irrigation

Onions are not demanding vegetables in terms of water, they are to be watered only when the soil is completely dry, taking care not to exaggerate as the roots of the onions are rather superficial and rot in case of stagnation. During the summer, above all, it is important to avoid that the soil dries up and hardens under the sun, therefore, it is to be regularly watered. In many cases a drip irrigation system is useful.

Insects harmful to onions

The onion fly is the insect that represents the biggest problem for this cultivation, to drive it away in a synergistic garden the best system is the association between carrots and onions, carrots in fact are natural repellents for this fly.

There are other pests that can damage our allium cepa crops, so we have published a guide dedicated to recognizing them and to fight them with only natural methods.

Picking and storing onions

Onions are a vegetable that can be kept practically all year round, provided you pick it at the right time and then know how to store it properly. Basically, we harvest using a period of dormancy of the bulb, which then remains idle without germinating for a few months.

If the onion is not kept properly it rots or germinates, trying to give birth to a new plant. In the latter case you can also choose to plant it, to get fresh onions.

Harvesting

The onions would be a biennial plant, in the garden is grown as annual avoiding the formation of seeds. In fact, the onions should be harvested without waiting for them to bloom.

We can understand that the onion is ready to be picked when the "cane" of its aerial part bends by itself. The harvesting period can also be understood by the yellowing of the stem. Harvesting must always be done before they start to mount in flower developing the floral scape. We also wait for the bulb to enlarge.

The onion bulb can always be harvested, in the sense that it is always edible, but you have to wait for the plant to dry out so that it can be kept for a long time. If we harvest it too early, its water content causes it to deteriorate prematurely and we are obliged to consume the onion within a few days. We must therefore wait for the plant to dry out, this is the right time to catch it and ensure it can be stored properly.

In the peasant tradition it is common practice to fold the onion plant manually before harvesting. In my opinion this work is useless, just wait for it to happen spontaneously. If someone has different opinions and above all different experiences, they can write about it in the comments.

The harvesting method is very simple: you remove the whole plant to take the bulb which is partially buried.

Conservation of the onion

For proper storage, as already mentioned, you must first seize at the right time. If you pick the unripe bulb even if it is then dried you will get onions ready to sprout at the first humidity, while if you pick at the right time the bulbs resist for the whole period of dormancy and keep for a long time in an excellent way.

As soon as they are picked, the onions dry for a day or two in the sun, then they should be stored in a cool, dark place, like garlic. Traditionally, the onions are tied together by the leaves by braiding, i.e. forming braids that hang in ventilated places, such as the porches of the farmsteads.

The dormancy, on which the preservation of the vegetable depends, varies in duration: 60-120 days depending on the variety, golden onions generally last longer, while red onions such onions are less durable. Therefore, red, and white onions are usually eaten fresh, while golden onions are kept longer for preservation. In a home garden it is therefore convenient to have different varieties to eat onions all year round.

In addition to dormancy, the enemy of conservation is rotting, which occurs in humid conditions. The fact that the bulbs are kept in a humid and ventilated place, as well as not placing them too much on top of each other in crates, helps to prevent the onions from mutating or rotting.

Oregano in pots

This medicinal plant can also be grown in pots, on the terrace or balcony, if we do not have a vegetable garden.

Being a plant that needs light and warmth, it can be cultivated indoors, in winter, to have fresh leaves with which to flavour dishes, in particular pizzas and tomato salads.

Also, for the potted soil it is advisable to aim at a fairly poor mixture, the common garden soil, mixed with a bit of sand, will do very well.

If you do not have an acquaintance or a friend who can provide you with two or three cuttings to have, in a short time, new plants, you can always resort to sowing, which, in a controlled environment such as that of a pot, will ensure the germination of several plants that will then be cut off.

The location of the oregano in pot must be well exposed to the sun and with regular but not abundant watering, in full summer.

Sowing period

If you decide to opt for sowing, the recommended period is spring or autumn, much depends on the altitude and regional climatic conditions.

Sowing is one of the possible sowing methods, although to better control other weeds, we recommend sowing in rows.

The seeds should be buried in furrows 30 cm apart and at a depth of 0,5 cm.

After germination, the seedlings should be cut into rows until a distance of about 30 cm between one seedling and the other is obtained.

Even if it is not a particularly decorative plant, if you have a rock garden you can place some seedlings in that place which, in all probability, will find an ideal location there.

When do you harvest oregano?

Given that the leaves can be eaten fresh, in any period of the vegetative phase, the actual harvest should take place before the flowers open, approximately in the period from the end of June to mid-August.

It is at this stage, in fact, that oregano concentrates the greatest quantity of aromatic substances and is therefore more fragrant.

These characteristics are important since the oregano cultivated in a specialized way is not only dried and chopped, to provide us with the preparation that we commonly find in supermarket jars, but also to obtain essential oils for liqueurs and for the pharmaceutical industry.

Parsnip

Here is a little-known but delicious vegetable, as well as easy to grow: the parsnip, also called white carrot.

The edible part of interest to the grower is the taproot that develops underground. The vegetable is eaten cooked: it is a vegetable with a soft paste and sweet taste, reminiscent of potatoes and carrots.

The parsnip is sown directly in the vegetable garden by placing its small seeds a few millimetres deep in the ground. Before putting the plant, however, it is important to choose the right place and work the soil properly. For root vegetables, as for the cultivation of tubers, the soil is a fundamental factor.

Where to grow parsnips

Climate. The parsnip plant is not afraid of frost, which in fact makes the taste of the root sweeter, but it loves the exposure to the sun, so it is best to plant it in areas of the garden not shaded.

The right soil. The soil in which to cultivate parsnips must be light and soft, there must be no water stagnation. Moreover, it would be better to choose a substratum that does not tend to compact too much. Also, a stony soil should be avoided: it can be an obstacle to the development of the root, being the part that interests us of this vegetable it is useful to take it into account.

Processing and fertilisation

We do not have the possibility to choose the land where to cultivate, so if the soil in our garden is not ideal for parsnips, we can work to improve it. Soils that are too clayey will have to be thoroughly and several times, we can also add river sand to lighten the texture. If the plot tends to accumulate water in stagnation you can decide to raise the cultivation bed to facilitate the flow of water thanks to the slope created.

Processing. In any case, it is essential to work the soil well so that it is loose and allows the root to swell without resistance, so a simple spading is not enough, but you have to till the soil of the garden several times reaching a depth of 40 cm, if possible. After the deeper tillage we proceed by hoeing the soil, in this phase it is also useful to fertilize, and finally we prepare the seedbed levelling with a rake.

Fertilization. To fertilize this crop, it is better to avoid using fresh manure or abounding with other nitrogen fertilizers: excesses of nitrogen may favour foliar development, to the detriment of root swelling. When working the soil, you can use mature manure or compost to be incorporated into the first 15 centimetres of soil. Wood ash containing potassium is very useful.

Sowing parsnip

The parsnip is sown between February and June directly in the open field. It is better to avoid passing through the seedbed, because the taproot risks deforming due to constriction in the container and tolerates transplanting badly. Sowing in the field is instead simple and fast, the seeds must be less than 2 cm deep. In the cultivation of this vegetable, germinating the seeds is usually the main rock, because they have a rather rigid external tegument.

Care must be taken because the seed has a short germination life and must therefore be of recent production, if the seed is more than two years old there is a risk of not seeing any seedlings born.

Since germination is quite difficult and it is advisable to soak the seeds one night before planting the parsnips in the garden. An interesting idea is to soak the seeds in chamomile tea.

Seeding depths and distances

How to sow the parsnip: the seed must be placed at a depth of 1 cm or 1.5 cm so that the seedling emerges easily. You can take into account that with 30/50 grams of seed you cover 100 square meters of cultivation. For a small family vegetable garden 5/6 square meters net cultivated with parsnips may be enough, at least as a taste the first time, and then adjust according to the tastes and consumption of the family.

Sixth planting: the parsnip is sown in rows 30/50 cm apart, placing the seeds 15 cm from each other. The right sowing distance is very important to ensure the right space at the root to develop. If you sow the parsnips too close together it is good to correct them during cultivation, thinning them out.

Cultivation operations

The cultivation of parsnips is simple, after sowing the most demanding work is the control of weeds. It is very useful to pass between the plants with a weeder, ideal the one recommended with the wheel, which allows you to do the job quickly. By weeding you get a double result: on the one hand you eliminate young wild plants, keeping them clean, on the other hand you move and oxygenate the soil, which is very important to make the root swell. As an alternative to weeding it is useful to mulch, an operation which is particularly convenient to do with straw.

When necessary, we intervene by irrigating, without ever exaggerating with water, whilst it is not necessary to fertilize again, seen that the cultivation is satisfied with little.

The parsnip can also be grown in a vase, although it is not particularly indicated because the container limits the development of the roots. It is necessary to use a big pot, to be filled with soil mixed with sand.

Parasites and adversities

Harmful insects. Parsnip sativa is a crop with the same parasites and problems that typically affect the carrot. Particular attention should be paid to ferrets and nematodes as pests, typical enemies of tuber and root crops, and the carrot fly.

Harvesting and storing sativa parsnips

Harvesting takes place in autumn or winter and is carried out by completely extracting the plant from the soil of the garden, since what is interesting to obtain is the large root. The sativa parsnip root is always edible, even if extracted young, but allowing it to swell obviously maximizes the quantity of production.

To understand when the time is right, you can observe the plant at the collar, at the limit inspecting the first centimetres of soil, to get an idea of the diameter of the vegetable, which develops deep underground.

If you wish, you can leave the plant in the ground for a long time, where it keeps perfectly, protecting it with a straw mulch. This is undoubtedly the best choice for family gardens, where you can make a scalar harvest, in relation to the needs.

The parsnip, as already written, can be harvested between autumn and winter, the winter one is generally better, because the frost turns starches into sugars. It is better to take this into account when planning the vegetable garden, in order to sow it to harvest it after the frosts, managing at the same time the spaces of the garden in the best way.

Conservation. After harvesting the parsnip, it must be left to dry, leaving it in a place where there is the right air circulation and average temperature, then it can be stored in dark, cool, and dry places.

How to cook parsnips

The parsnip can be eaten raw by grating it like carrots, but its best expression is if it is cooked like a potato. To prepare it, we must first clean it and peel it. We can cook it in the oven, fried, sautéed, steamed, or boiled.

In England, parsnip sativa parsnips are also used to make an alcoholic beverage, through fermentation, called parsnip wine.

From a nutritional point of view, it is a vegetable particularly rich in fibre and contains various useful elements such as copper, potassium, magnesium, and vitamin C. It is a food that satiates a lot. So, it can be a side dish of substance, when not main course.

Peas in pots

The pea (Pisum sativum) is one of those plants which lends itself well to be cultivated also in pots, without cares if not those required also by plants cultivated in the ground.

Belonging to the family of leguminous plants, the pea presents itself, during flowering, with elegant white flowers that will then develop green pods containing from 7 to 10 seeds each.

The peas with shells, which we normally buy in supermarkets, can therefore be very fresh, directly at home once they go into production.

When and how to sow the peas in pots

The peas can be sown in autumn (October-November) or in winter, usually in February, when the temperature has reached 5-6 degrees.

The pea plant is characterized by having important roots and, consequently, it is necessary to prepare suitable containers that can guarantee its correct development.

It is essential to sow in large containers that are at least 50cm deep.

The seeds should be placed at about 3 or 4 cm from each other, on a single groove in the centre of the pot, burying them for about 3-4 cm.

The choice of soil

The ideal soil for sowing peas must be fresh, i.e. light, and moist at the same time.

Do not worry, you do not need particularly fertilised or nitrogen-rich soil, but the physical qualities of the soil written above deserve to invest some resources.

The rule of crop rotation in the open field also applies to potted pea sowing.

If, however, you do not have to sow the peas on the same plot for more than two or three consecutive years in the open field, it is highly recommended that you do not use the same soil in which the peas were planted in the previous year.

Changing the growing medium serves to prevent plant diseases.

How much water to give the peas

This plant needs regular watering although, just like many other plants, we should avoid excesses which, during hot humid periods, can favour the development of fungal diseases.

The golden rule to avoid water stagnations and to avoid that the roots enter and remain in contact with the water for too long, consists in placing on the bottom of the pot a layer of draining material such as expanded clay.

Watering can be reduced if we take care to protect the surface of the soil with mulch, or a cloth under which to install a drip irrigation system.

Placement and exposure of the pots

The vases (or the raised bed) should be placed in areas that are bright and not excessively exposed. Windbreak panels to be combined with large planters would be the ideal condition, also to create the ideal support for the plants.

If the pot/flowerpot is large enough, you can also consider the possibility of combining the cultivation of peas with that of other vegetables.

The vegetables that go best with peas are carrots, lettuce and even beans, while it is not advisable to combine them with garlic.

Growing advices

As mentioned, because of the puny structure of the drums, the peas need support to climb on.

I mentioned above the windbreak panels (better the half-timbered ones), but you can also use nets or more rustic reeds.

This aspect, in an urban context, can also have useful implications, both on the ornamental front and on the privacy that the vegetation cover can guarantee.

On the other hand, it is necessary to be aware that, where robust wind-break panels are not used, there is a risk that strong winds can cause damage, finding a mild resistance in the pea supports.

For reasons of practicality, it is perhaps better to focus on dwarf varieties that do not require any kind of support.

Peppers

The pepper is an interesting vegetable for the various uses it can have in the kitchen, it is a plant quite demanding in terms of nutrients but also gives great satisfaction at harvest time. As a vegetable to be grown in the garden is very common, in gardens you can find both sweet pepper and chilli, the latter is also grown a lot indoors or on the balcony.

Soil. The pepper plant requires soil ideally with a pH value between 5.5 and 7, rich in organic matter and possibly sandy. The preparation of the soil for the peppers requires a deep spading (even 40-50 cm if possible) to facilitate water drainage. It is very important that the soil does not facilitate stagnation to prevent plant diseases.

Fertilisation. Peppers like soil rich in organic matter, so they need 3-6 kg of mature manure or a tenth if pelleted organic manure (manure or pollen) is used. If you have a choice, it is always better to provide natural soil improver organic manure, such as compost and manure, rather than the dried pellet equivalent.

Climatic conditions. The climate suitable for peppers depends very much on the variety chosen, some need higher temperatures. In general, it is a vegetable that prefers mild temperatures and hot summers. Good exposure is recommended, although excessive sunshine in summer on some varieties can burn the fruit.

Sowing. Pepper seeds need high temperatures to germinate, so the advice is to plant the seeds in the seedbed in a warm bed (you can use a cable or a mat to heat the seedbed). With a temperature of 24-26 degrees the seeds will be born within about ten days, you can accelerate them with a chamomile bath if necessary. You sow in winter to have the seedlings ready in spring.

The Cultivation

Braces. The pepper has a plant that requires to be supported with braces to the various branches, so as not to bend and support the weight of the fruit. You can also use a 10 x 10 square mesh net to be spread 50 cm high horizontally. The larger the size of the fruit, the more important it is to make the supports.

Pruning. In the sweet pepper, in order to obtain a harvest of good size, the plant must be pruned to eliminate some fruits, concentrating energy on the remaining ones. The pepper plant begins with a flower, then increases exponentially, in fact it goes on forking and each bifurcation in turn is divided in two. As the fruit production increases, the size is gradually reduced and pruning always eliminates one of the two forks. In this way we obtain a similar production if we measure the weight but distributed on fruits of homogeneous size.

Irrigation. The peppers have an increasing need for water, which increases as the fruits appear, so there is no need for irrigation.

Growing peppers and chillies in pots

The peppers are also very suitable for balcony gardens, growing in pots, with the possibility to have fruit until autumn and many hot peppers to dry all winter. For the cultivation in pot, it is better to use a container of quite large size (depth and diameter at least 30 cm), preparing a layer of expanded clay at the bottom of the pot. We also use generic soil, with the addition of mature compost or earthworm humus.

The shrewdness to have is to irrigate frequently and to return to fertilize a little during the cultivation cycle. We can do this with a handful of pelleted manure, but also with nettle macerate.

When to harvest the peppers

As for the tomato, also for the pepper the ripening process takes place in two stages: first the seeds and the inner part ripen, then the outer part. If the skin is still green it means that the process has not yet been completed. As soon as the fruits reach optimal size and degree of ripeness, they must always be removed from the plant, to encourage the development of the other fruits.

Normally the peppers start to ripen after about 60 days from the fruit set, but they complete their colouring after 80 - 100 days, always counted from the setting of the flower. If the fruit is harvested as soon as it begins to turn, it can be completed after 2 - 3 days, but it will wither all the faster the greener it was initially.

For food purposes, the difference between a green fruit and a coloured one is minimal, simply the green contains less lycopene, we try to obtain uniformly coloured peppers for aesthetic purposes, very important in professional cultivation.

Pepper pests

Even parasites can bring serious problems to our pepper cultivation, there are organic methods that can be useful to fight harmful insects, without poisoning the vegetable and the environment.

Aphids. As with most garden plants, peppers can also be attacked by aphids, the danger of these lice is mainly due to the possibility that they transmit viruses to the plant. In case of attack there are several natural methods, from Marseille soap to neem oil, to learn more you can read more about the defence against aphids.

Red spider mite. This small insect is a parasite that brings dwarfism, defoliation or lack of production of the pepper plant, to combat the red spider can use the wettable sulfur, to be sprayed in the cooler hours, although it is a treatment that maintains a certain toxicity, although it is allowed in the organic. A more natural method is the use of garlic macerate.

Trialeurodes. This insect is also called white fly, it attacks the pepper especially when grown in greenhouses, I dedicated a post to how to defend against Trialeurodes.

Pyrrhoid. Insect of the lepidoptera family that lays its eggs on the pepper. It loves corn above all, a crop that attracts the pyrrhoids, so if there is corn grown around the garden the peppers can suffer substantial attacks. The new born larva pierces the skin and eats the fruit, ruining it and encouraging rotting, especially if rain follows. The borer can be fought with bacillus thuringiensis, which kills the larvae but is a selective insecticide.

Potatoes

This tuber certainly needs no introduction: we are talking about one of the most important vegetables among those grown, because of its great use in the kitchen.

The optimal soil for growing potatoes should have a pH of around 6 (you can read how to measure the pH of the soil), however, less than 7. It is necessary to prepare a good background fertilization: indicatively it is better to use around 6 kg of mature manure per square meter or 0.6 kg if we use manure or pelleted manure, when it is possible better to lean for manure rather than using dried fertilizers. The tillage must be deep, in order to offer now of sowing a loose and very draining soil, for this reason it is spat out by sinking the blade up to 30/40 cm. The potato plant fears water stagnation, which would cause the tubers to rot.

Sowing potatoes

The potatoes are sown from spring, average temperatures must be over 10 degrees, ideally between 12 and 20 degrees. Depending on the climate zone, the planting period can vary between February and June, where the winter is very mild, you can also sow in autumn in September/October.

The sixth planting period involves sowing in rows, spaced 70 cm apart. One potato is placed every 25-30 cm along each row, buried at a depth of 10 cm. Alternatively you can also put the potato on the surface and then cover it with 10 cm of soil, so that the plant benefits from the softer part of the soil. The technique is particularly useful with very compact or moist soil.

Sowing potatoes is a multiplication by cuttings: the real seed is contained in the green balls that follow the flowering, while the tuber is a modified stem that acts as a starch reserve for the plant. When sowing by cutting you can use whole potatoes but also pieces of tuber. If the size exceeds 50 grams in fact, we can divide the tuber to have more seed. The important thing is that each piece is at least 20 grams and has a minimum of two "eyes" (the buds), the cut must be made in segments, not dividing in half, since most of the buds are on the pole opposite the stolon. To see the buds better, you can put the potatoes in a warm place and moisten them every two days, after a week the shoots will stretch up to 1-2 cm and you can proceed to the partitioning of the tubers. Care must be taken not to damage the newborn shoots when planting. After cutting, leave to dry for a few days for the potatoes to heal, after which the potatoes are planted. The position of the potato on the ground does not matter.

Potato cultivation

To grow potatoes in the garden there are relatively few precautions to be taken: once the tubers have been planted in a well tilled and well fertilised soil, the crop requires irrigation only when necessary and control by adversity and insects, which we will discuss in the dedicated paragraph. The most important work during cultivation is tamping, which also eliminates most weeds.

Tamping potatoes

First tuck. After 15 - 20 days from sowing the first two real leaves will sprout, the shoots will be damaged in case of frost, so it is better to bury the two small leaves with a slight tamping, to be done when at least half of the plants have emitted the leaves. The advantage is also to eliminate the first weeds and force the plant to lengthen the stem, thus increasing the production of stolon's and therefore potatoes.

Second tamping. After one month, a further tamping will be carried out, distributing a fertilizer before the tamping operation. In this way, a pile of about 30 centimetres is created on the plant, which protects the tubers from the sun. The direct light causes the production of solanine which is a poisonous substance, the potatoes with the sun's rays turn green and are not edible.

Irrigation

Usually for the potato, there are two types of irrigation: flow or rain, the best time is early in the morning, the time of day with cooler temperatures. The attention to the temperatures is important to prevent diseases of the plant: at 18° C the downy mildew already starts to act, in order not to favour it better to irrigate early. The periods when more water is required during the cultivation of the potato are when the buds appear and then at the end of flowering.

Fertilization

The potato is a demanding vegetable and requires excellent bottom fertilisation, but it can also be fertilised during sowing and then during the entire first period of growth. To learn more about this we recommend reading the article dedicated to how and how much to fertilize potatoes.

Yield and harvest

Productivity. Normally the yield of product in a potato field is 3-4 kg of tubers per square metre of cultivated land, so that the amount of space to be devoted to this crop can be calculated in the home garden in relation to family consumption.

The time of harvest. If you want new potatoes, you must harvest the potatoes when the plant is still green, while normal potatoes, which are also suitable for storage, are harvested once the plant dries out and turns completely yellow. At this point the tuber is perfectly formed. The ripening time changes according to the variety of potatoes sown, the climatic conditions of the locality and the vintage, the easiest way to know when it is time to harvest the potatoes is to sample by harvesting a plant.

How to understand ripening. To understand if a potato is ready just rub the peel: if it does not come off easily it means that it is time to harvest the potatoes. Potatoes are in any case edible even before, in the family garden you can then make a scalar harvest, only the well ripe potato, however, can be kept for months without problems. See the section on potato harvesting in more detail.

How to harvest. The harvesting operation is carried out with gallows, lifting the clod of soil under the plant, and finding all the tubers formed at the roots.

Insects and pests

If we plant potatoes in our garden, we must be ready to recognise insects and pests that can damage our plants. Combating them by natural means is possible but requires prompt action at the first occurrence of the infestation. Let us see what the main enemies of the potato are.

Aphids or potato lice. Aphids are insects that you find on the leaves and can transmit virosis to the plant. They are fought with natural methods such as garlic, propolis, nettle macerate, or pyrethrum, an insecticide allowed by organic farming. The latter product also kills bees and although natural, it is toxic, so it is best used with caution. Learn more: defend against aphids.

Dorifora. This beetle attack potato, is fought with controls and manual removal, paying attention in mid-May. Learn more: eliminate the dorifora.

Elaterides: they are underground worms that feed on roots and tubers and are prevented by mulching and crop rotation. Learn more: the Elaterides.

Gryllotalpa: is a large insect (5-6 cm) that digs and feeds on tubers and roots. It can be fought by placing traps along tunnels, or it can be prevented by destroying nests. Learn more about it: the fight against the mole Gryllotalpa.

Other problems of potato cultivation in the garden that are not related to insects are weed, a weed that pierces the tubers. Care should also be taken if there are pieces of glass or sheet metal in the soil that could be embedded in the tuber.

Storing potatoes

The potatoes should be stored in the dark so that they do not produce solanine, which makes them inedible. The presence of excessive solanine can be recognised by the green colour of the tuber from the outside.

Between the harvesting of the potatoes and the appearance of the sprouts there is the period of dormancy. This period varies between 70 and 120 days, depending on the variety of potato used (this has nothing to do with earliness). This is useful information, which should be indicated on the seed bag. The ideal in the garden is to plant the potatoes at different times, according to the needs of consumption. The dormancy increases if the tubers are stored in the cold (temperatures of 1/5 degrees), but in this way a large part of the starch is transformed into sugars, so before consumption it is necessary to bring the potato back to room temperature for a week by reversing the process.

Pumpkin

Pumpkin is a vegetable that should not be missing in the garden, given the generous production of vegetables it guarantees.

In addition to the pumpkin that is cooked the plant is sometimes grown to make ornamental pumpkins, which are dug and used as a container or as a Halloween lantern, there is also a kind of pumpkin from which to make a natural sponge, the luffa.

Climate. The pumpkin is afraid of frost and is damaged at temperatures below 10 degrees, the plant suffers even if it is too hot, over 30 degrees. Ideal for growing it in the garden is a mild temperature, around 20 degrees. In the more torrid summer months, it can be useful to use shading nets.

Soil and fertilizer. The pumpkin needs a rich soil, with a pH value ideally between 6 and 7. To get quality pumpkins to compost or mature manure, you need to add a lot of potassium, which makes the fruit tastier and sweeter, so it is excellent to mix ash at will in the compost, or use "borlande" (beet processing residues, found in agricultural centres among the natural fertilizers). The pumpkin is really very demanding in terms of fertilization: before growing it, you can dig a hole to be filled with manure, preparing this bed of nourishment, or bury 3 or 4 quintals of manure every 100 square meters of garden.

Sowing the pumpkin

How and when to sow. The pumpkin can be sown directly in the garden, alternatively the seedlings can be grown in pots. In the seedbed you sow from mid-April and then transplant from the end of the month, for pumpkin seedlings it is better to use large jars, I recommend a diameter of 8 cm. If you sow directly in the field, you can make small posts in which you put 3-4 seeds. Our advice is to raise the posts slightly above ground level, even if only 10 cm is enough. To learn more about times and ways you can read the guide to sowing pumpkin.

Sixth of planting. Pumpkin plants have a great horizontal development, that is why they are planted in groups of two, close to each other and each one goes in a different direction. This saves manure and space and optimises the garden. The distances to plant the pumpkins in the field must be well spaced: we are talking about 160 or 200 cm between plants.

Growing of pumpkins

Pumpkin is a demanding vegetable but not particularly difficult to grow, with a few simple tips that I list below you will have excellent results.

Thin the seedlings. When the seedlings have 3 or 4 real leaves they thin out, leaving the best of each post.

Hoeing and weeding. Pumpkin plants love the soil to be moved and well oxygenated, that is why it is a useful system to periodically hoe the flowerbed of the garden cultivated with pumpkin. In addition to hoeing, you can also bury a bit of fertiliser before flowering and possibly tamp the plants down. Hoeing not only moves the soil with the hoe, but also controls weeds.

Nettle macerate. Nettle macerate is an excellent organic fertilizer for young pumpkin seedlings, to be sprayed after transplanting, diluted in water with a ratio of 1 to 5. Those who want to obtain giant pumpkins above all will have to take care to provide nutrients even after the transplant, which is in progress. As liquid fertilizer the nettle macerate is positive to be used during the cultivation, while the organic substance is better to put it before, during the soil tillage.

Irrigation and mulching

Irrigation. The pumpkin requires water, especially when it starts to bloom. You do not have to water it often, but you need to provide plenty of water so that it can penetrate deep into the soil. However, it is important to make sure you do not let excess water stagnate, if it does, it could cause disease.

Mulching. Since the pumpkin is going to lie on the ground, it is a good idea to use mulching. This way the fruit does not rest directly on the ground and you save a lot of weed weeding work. If you do not mulch the weeds have to be carefully removed and you can put weeds under the fruit, so that when the soil is damp, there is no rot. In addition, there are small worms, the Elaterides, which could eat the fruit if it is placed on the ground.

Pruning: prune the pumpkin

The topping of the branch is carried out periodically and is an important pruning work to balance the plant and direct its resources towards the formation of the fruit. To prune the pumpkin, it is necessary to cut after the second or fourth leaf (depending on how developed the plant is). The purpose of this pruning is to produce axillary shoots, which will bring production, if instead you want large pumpkins better intervene differently, leaving only a couple of fruits.

Pumpkin harvesting

Fruit picking. The pumpkin is harvested when it is perfectly ripe, only with the ripening it becomes sweeter and tastier and keeps longer, unlike the zucchini that is instead harvested unripe. The ripe pumpkin can be recognized when the skin is very hard, and you cannot scratch it with your fingernail. We recommend a more in-depth study on how to understand when to pick the pumpkin, since understanding the right moment is one of the great dilemmas of the garden. There you will find some useful tricks.

To keep the pumpkins harvested you must keep them in a cool and dry place, be careful to put them in the cellar because it is often too humid. Once harvested, the pumpkins fear the excessive cold, which can crystallize the pulp.

Pumpkin flowers

The pumpkin flower is very good eaten fried in batter or stir-fried in risotto. The flowers can be picked considering not to stop pollination, otherwise you lose the harvest of the fruit. The advice is not to harvest in the morning but after midday and to harvest only the male flowers, recognizable by the elongated "petiole". You will also find a post that explains better when to pick the pumpkin flowers so as not to lose even one fruit.

Pumpkin seeds

With the aim of wasting as little as possible and discovering different flavours, every part of the pumpkin can be used: even seeds dried and roasted are an excellent salty snack, to be eaten as an aperitif. They can also be put in salads to flavour with a crunchy element.

Radishes

It is a plant quite resistant to pest attacks, with a short cultivation cycle (usually around 30 days).

Climate. The climate must not be too hot, the radish loves a good sun exposure but a temperate or cool climate.

Type of soil. The radish plant requires a loose and draining soil, better if calcareous. To grow it in vegetable gardens with compact and heavy soil, sand must be added a couple of months before sowing.

Fertilization and vegetable garden tillage. The soil must be well tilled, going as far as to spade in depth, the fertilizer should be used in moderation, taking into account that an excess of nitrogen causes the growth of the aerial part of the plant, to the detriment of the root which is what interests the horticulturist.

The sowing of radishes

Sowing period. The radishes can be sown from the beginning of spring until the end of summer, a cultivation cycle of 30-40 days is taken into account depending on the variety, so it is possible to plan the sowing to harvest in a scalar manner according to consumption.

How to sow. The radishes are sown directly in the ground, planting the seed in the garden at a depth of about one centimetre.

Sixth of planting. Generally, the radish is cultivated in rows 20 cm apart, with distances of 4/5 cm between the seedlings. It is also possible to sow by spreading the seeds and then thinning the plants later.

How to grow them in the organic garden and when to harvest them

Thin it. It is a plant that germinates quickly, after about ten days the radish seedlings are thinned out so that each root finds its proper space. The distance to leave is at least 3 cm, if the variety has large roots it will thin out to 5-6 cm between the plants.

Irrigation. The radish requires a constant and balanced amount of water: too much irrigation causes an important foliar growth but with little development of the root, the lack of water makes the root woody and spicy in taste.

Weeding and hoeing. The radishes in the garden must be kept clean from weeds with weeding. The soil must then be hoed periodically in order to ventilate and make the soil soft.

Harvesting. The radish is harvested about a month after sowing, winter ones take longer, even two months. If the root remains in the soil for a long time, it hardens and becomes spicy.

Subsociation. Radish goes well with all vegetables, being also an undemanding plant. It is only suggested not to let other cruciferous plants happen. It is said that the combination with lettuce improves the taste of radish making it less spicy.

Enemies and Diseases

The radish is attacked by the same parasites that affect the vegetables of its family, so the insects to be careful of are the same ones that affect the cabbage, they are Gryllotalpa and aphids.

Particularly annoying to radishes are the nettles, or land fleas that pierce the leaves and compromise the harvest. While the larvae of the nettles erode the underground part, the adult beetles eat the aerial part. At the first sightings, it is necessary to kill the nettles with pyrethrum.

Due to the short crop cycle, fungal diseases such as downy mildew or fusarium usually do no great damage to the radish.

Rhubarb

The rhubarb plant (rheum rhaponticum or rheum rhabarbarum, of the polygonises family) is a polyannual herbaceous plant that forms a large taproot, from this rhizome starts the secondary root system and on it are present the buds from which the ribs and leaves are born. It is found widespread wild throughout Europe and part of Asia, the wild rhubarb is edible just like the one we can grow, selected to have stems of better size. The rhubarb stems take on a colour between light green and bright red, but they can also be white or yellowish depending on the variety, while the leaves are large and emerald green. The amount of oxalic acid in the leaves makes them inedible, while the ribs can be eaten without contraindication. In April, the rheum emits a floral scape that rises like a plume and then reveals an explosion of white flowers. The flower then gives way to the fruit, small nuts containing the seeds.

It is a good-looking plant, especially because of the bright colour of the stems and the large size of the flower, interesting to be inserted in cultivated plots and often used also for ornamental purposes and not only for the edibility of the coasts: it does not disfigure in the garden.

From the cultivation point of view, rhubarb is a polyannual plant, which does not have to be sown every year and requires very little care. It produces for a good period of the year, in the mild climate zones.

Chinese rhubarb. In addition to rheum rhaponticum, rheum palmatum, which is called Chinese rhubarb, is also cultivated. It is a very similar herbaceous species with similar food uses and the same cultivation method.

The giant rhubarb. There is then another plant called "giant rhubarb", a well-deserved epithet, as it reaches the 2 metres of height.

Where to grow rhubarb

Climatic requirements. The rhubarb plant does not like the heat, not for nothing is characteristic of northern Europe and can also be grown in mountain gardens, but it lives very well in the Italian climate. However, a moderate temperature allows a longer period of production and therefore a greater harvest. In central and southern Italy, where it suffers the most from the torrid summer, it can be better off in half-light than in full sunshine. On the other hand, it resists the winter without any problem, being in vegetative stasis in the coldest months. When you see the coasts and leaves deteriorate and dry out in autumn, you do not have to despair: the root system remains alive in the soil and vigorous shoots will come back in spring.

Suitable soil. Rhubarb does not require much from the soil, although it loves organic matter and nitrogen. Before planting it is good to prepare a background fertilization, as it is a perennial plant it is better to leave nourishment that can be absorbed even after the first year, so to prefer manure or compost rather than dry pelleted manure, very well also put mineral flours. Like many other vegetables, rhubarb does not like water stagnations, so it must be cultivated on draining soil.

The importance of drainage and processing. Before sowing or transplanting this crop, it is a good idea to work thoroughly with the spade on the dedicated garden plot, so that its rhizome can develop comfortably in a soft substrate. The water must drain off easily because if it stagnates, creating a soggy and muddy soil around the roots would favour rottenness, which leads to the death of the plant. In soils that are particularly prone to compacting or in any case not very draining, it is advisable to create raised cultivation beds with lateral drainage channels. It can also be considered to use sand to make the soil more draining.

Reproduction of rhubarb

Rhubarb can be reproduced in two ways: sowing and rhizome partition (agamic multiplication). The second method is undoubtedly the easiest to implement and the fastest. After sowing or multiplying it will be easy to plant it.

Sowing rhubarb

Start with the seed. Rhubarb can be grown from seed, the seed is planted in pots at the beginning of March, then transplanted in mid-April or May outdoors in the garden. If you start from seed, the plant will produce from the second or third year, so a little patience is needed compared to transplanting, which is faster in harvesting.

Transplanting the seedling. If you buy a seedling or if you get it by sowing it in the seedbed, the best time for transplanting is usually mid-April or even May, it is not excluded that rhubarb can also tolerate other periods for planting, being very resistant. After transplanting remember to water regularly and during the first months of life to control weeds.

Division of rhizomes

The best way to multiply rhubarb plants is to plant one and divide the head into several parts: each piece can be buried and will give birth to a new plant. The important thing is to make sure that each piece of rhizome has at least one bud. This can be done in early spring or before winter. If you have a rhubarb plant available it is certainly the best way to expand your cultivation.

Distance between plants

The rheum is a really vigorous plant, which expands and produces large leaves, for this reason it is advisable to keep a good distance between the rhubarb plants, I suggest to leave as a planting sixth two meters between one row and the other and at least one meter between the plants. In the family garden, however, you will not need more than two or three plants, unless you want to make rhubarb jams often! Only one rhubarb plant produces a good number of ribs. When growing in pots, of course, you only put one plant per container.

Work to do

Cleaning weeds in the rhubarb area is easy, its large leaves grow quickly and provide shade by limiting weeds. If mulching is used, the weeding work becomes practically zero. Weeds are to be cared for especially in the first period of the rhubarb's life, when the seedlings are still small, once the plant has grown competes well. However, weeding the soil is positive regardless, because it breaks the surface crust and allows the soil to oxygenate.

The green mulch of clover

An interesting technique that combines the merits of mulching with those of the synergy between crops is the green live mulching, it is to sow clover dwarf to create a covering carpet of soil around the rhubarb plants. The small roots of clover bring nitrogen to the soil and thus enrich it with a very useful element to rheum, at the same time avoiding the growth of weeds and helping to retain water in the soil.

Irrigation

When the plant is young it is necessary to take care that the soil is always damp, once the rhizome develops and the root system increases in size we should intervene only in case of dry weather and prolonged lack of rain. In any case, when irrigating the rhubarb, it is necessary to be careful not to exaggerate, if lasting stagnations are provoked rottenness which can make the plant die. The potted plant should be irrigated more often, with small amounts of water each time.

Fertilization

The rhubarb is a perennial herbaceous plant, if we pick up the coasts, we go to subtract nutrients, so we must not lose fertility bring back organic matter and nutrients. We must therefore fertilize at least once a year; the late autumn is a good time to do so.

Nitrogen is, of course, one of the important nutrients to increase the harvest, so let us take this into account when deciding how to fertilise. We therefore use manure, mature compost, humus, or pelleted manure, to be hoeed lightly into the soil making it available to the root system of the plant. If we grow in pots it is best to fertilize at least three times a year, giving preference to pelleted or liquid fertilizer.

Flowering and flower cutting

Flowering requires a lot of energy from the plant, which otherwise would be destined to the production of ribs and leaves, which is why those who grow rhubarb as a vegetable should cut the floral scape as soon as it appears. Obviously, if you want the plant to form seeds to be able to reproduce it in that way, or if you are interested in the ornamental aspect of this large flowering plume, you will have to let its flower grow. The rhubarb flowers are very small, white, or yellowish, gathered in a nice sized spike.

Diseases and parasites of rhubarb

Rhubarb is a plant subject to few adversities. The most common diseases are root rot due to water stagnation, so as already explained they are prevented by ensuring good drainage of the soil.

Also, as insects there are generally no major problems. The wide leaves of rhubarb are an excellent shelter for slugs and snails, these do not worry much about rhubarb, even if they eat some leaves not bad: due to the content of oxalic acid are not suitable for human consumption. Let us worry rather about the fact that the gastropods hide in the shade of the rhubarb and then go out in the evening to eat the other vegetables.

Forcing rhubarb

Forcing is a cultivation technique that makes it possible to increase the quality of the rhubarb coasts and to anticipate production. It consists in keeping the rhubarb covered, special terracotta bells can be used for this purpose.

The covering on the one hand increases the temperature and therefore can bring an earlier harvest in spring and even later in autumn, but above all by removing photosynthesis it makes the stem softer and tastier and concentrates the substances more in the coasts, to the detriment of the leaf.

Rhubarb can be forced thanks to the fact that this perennial plant has a rhizome capable of accumulating a lot of energy, so even without light it can emit shoots and develop the aerial part of the plant. The cover is maintained for about 10/15 days, enough time to inhibit chlorophyll. After this period, we can open it, because in any case the rhubarb, like all plants, needs light to live.

Harvesting

Rhubarb is harvested from April until autumn, suspending in the summer heat so as not to make the plant suffer. When the cold weather arrives, a last harvest is made by cutting all the coasts. It is advisable to harvest the thicker stalks: avoiding looting the whole plant, leave one leaf in three. To pick rhubarb you take the coast and cut it at the base (the closer to the ground the better).

The stem is always edible, obviously the bigger it gets the more kg of crop we can get, optimizing productivity. Rhubarb is consumed only the coast, the leaves contain oxalic acid, which makes them toxic. If you start from the seed, the harvest will start from the second year, because the seedling is too small before.

Using rhubarb

Rhubarb is a plant with many uses, the root is used for herbs and liqueurs, the ribs are excellent in many vegan recipes and desserts. It is a healthy vegetable, containing various elements useful for the well-being of the body, such as iron, magnesium, and potassium. Be careful, however, that not the whole plant can be eaten: the leaves are toxic due to the content of oxalic acid.

Root and medicinal use

Rhubarb root can be used to make liqueurs, particularly rhubarb bitter. Root extract is also used for candy. Because of its properties, useful for the intestine, the root is used in herbal medicine and is also present in some medicines. Harvesting the root is always a shame because it is necessary to plant a plant that would be herbaceous perennial. If, however, we keep part of the rhizome, equipped with buds, we can then plant it again.

Making sweets and jams

The taste of rhubarb is difficult to describe in words, it has a fruity and strong taste, quite sweet, tending to acid. The rhubarb ribs are mainly used in desserts, especially in apple pies. You can make excellent rhubarb jams, very good jam in combination with strawberries. Other interesting uses are a sweet and sour chutney to be combined with meat and cheese and an elderberry-like syrup.

Spinach

Spinach are extremely interesting vegetables to grow in the garden, also because they grow quickly and resist the cold, allowing you to exploit the garden in less favourable periods such as late autumn.

The spinach is a species of the family of Chenopodiaceae, a relative of beets and beetroot, its botanical name is "spinacia oleracea" and is a plant native to Asia, although it is known and cultivated in Europe for centuries.

It is a small herbaceous plant, characterized by rosette leaves, which are also the harvested part, is cultivated on an annual cycle and is a species fast enough to grow.

Spinach does not ask a lot from the soil of the garden: it is important only that they have available a tilled soil so that it drains the excess water, this vegetable has no particular demands and can easily exploit the residual fertility left by other fertilized crops. It prefers a pH above 6.5.

Beware of excess nitrogen: do not use many nitrate fertilisers because spinach tends to accumulate in the leaf and becomes slightly toxic for these nitrates.

Growing spinach requires a cool climate, which is why it is best to grow it in spring or autumn. Spinach oleracea is a species that can easily withstand low temperatures, up to 5 degrees, while the heat of summer can cause a pre-flowering that ruins the harvest.

Spinach seedlings also have no problem staying in rather shady flowerbeds, on the contrary, it prefers half-shade rather than summer sun.

Soil preparation and fertilization

Preparing the soil for spinach requires, as with any vegetable, a good spading that reaches as deep as possible.

Then you can decide whether to spread organic manure, it is not necessary if you already have rich soil and if you have fertilized for earlier crops. In any case, excesses of nitrogen should be avoided, so do not overdo it with manure or other nitrogen fertilisers.

After digging, the soil is hoed, also incorporating any fertilizer, and finally it is levelled well with an iron rake, which smoothes and refines preparing the soil for sowing.

Planting or sowing spinach in the garden

We can decide to grow spinach either by direct sowing or by taking already formed seedlings. Personally, I suggest starting from the seed because it is cheaper, to buy the seedling on a fast-growing crop such as spinach is not very convenient.

Seeding period. Spinach can be grown practically all year round. They are usually sown in spring (March/April), for harvests before the summer, or in September to have them in autumn. It is best to avoid them in the field during the warmer months, when they would require frequent irrigation and shading nets.

Transplanting period. Even if you want to transplant, the ideal is to do it in April or September.

Planting season. Spinach plants should be in rows 40 cm apart, with plants every 15 cm. Since the seeds are small, it is best to sow at 5 cm and then thin out the plants as soon as they have grown, leaving about one plant in three. The seed is placed at a shallow depth, just 1 cm from the ground.

We can also choose to sow thicker and often harvest the leaves, this is indicated especially if we want to take small leaves, to eat tender. Even if you decide to thin out, you can do it with a formed plant, so that you can then eat the removed seedlings in a salad.

Irrigation and mulching

Spinach is a species which does not like drought, so it is good to irrigate when needed, possibly without wetting the leaves but pouring the water on the ground. Depending on the season, the necessary water supply can vary decidedly, in any case, it is good to prefer frequent irrigations with little water, rather than administering large quantities of water.

Harvest

You eat spinach leaves, which you can eat at any time. The young leaves are softer, also suitable to be eaten raw in salads, while the more developed leaves are more productive and can be eaten cooked in a pan.

If we want a good continuous production, we cut the larger leaves that grow on the sides, leaving the central head. If you want to cut the whole head it is advisable to cut it a little high, thus leaving the plant the possibility to harvest more than one crop.

Variety of spinach

There are different varieties of spinach, some cultivars are more suitable for spring and others for autumn cultivation.

Here are some recommended species:

Spinach Matador. Varieties with large, deep green leaves, among the most common in vegetable gardens. It produces a lot and is early, perfect both for winter and summer sowing.

Spinach Butterfly. It is a spinach with lanceolate leaves, resistant to cold and late flowering. For these characteristics it is excellent as autumn sowing spinach.

Spinach Verdil. Also, this spinach is not afraid of frost, it grows quickly and for this reason it is also good for winter cultivation.

Giant winter spinach. Dark, large, fleshy, smooth leaves. It is sown in October to harvest in the middle of winter.

Tomatoes

The tomatoes must be sown around the beginning of February.

Sowing must be carried out in a germinator heated to a temperature of 15-18 C°, or indoors behind a window exposed to the sun.

The tomatoes can also be sown at home in special containers but, in this case, it must be considered that the seedlings must be kept inside until transplanting outdoors is possible.

The advice is to sow in pots of about 7-10 centimetres in diameter so that the plant develops individually in its earth bread. In each jar place about three seeds spaced out from each other and once the seedlings will be 3 or 4 centimetres high you will choose the strongest one and you will eliminate the others so that you will have only one plant per jar.

To distribute the seeds correctly, it is advisable to harvest them in a sheet of paper folded in "V" and drop them, one by one, in the desired position, using the tip of a pencil.

To sow the tomatoes, use a soil suitable for seeds and sift over the seeds a layer of 0.50 cm of soil. Always keep the soil moist.

As we said, sowing in jars is the most convenient because, if we sow in boxes, we should then carry out additional transplanting work in the jars as soon as the first leaves have appeared. In jars, on the contrary, tomato plants will be able to develop undisturbed until the moment of their final transplanting in the garden.

At the beginning of April, the invigorating phase of the seedlings can begin in order to prepare them, little by little, for their definitive external environment.

Tomatoes are plants that need a lot of light and heat to be able to produce and bring their juicy fruits to maturity.

When you are about to transplant tomatoes you must choose, therefore, a position inside the garden well exposed to the sun trying to avoid, at the same time, to place the tomatoes in the same place of the previous year but, on the contrary, always follow the good rule of crop rotation to avoid diseases and not impoverish the soil with the same crops for several years.

The soil should be well tilled and a certain amount of well-ripened or garden compound should be added.

When the danger of night frosts is definitely averted, you can plant the tomato seedlings taking care not to damage the soil bread in which the roots have developed; to do this, never pull the tomato seedlings by taking their stem between your fingers but turn the pot upside down by holding the stem of the seedling between your fingers arranged in a "V".

After having dug a hole where we want to bury the seedling, place the roots and the soil bread so that it is buried 1.5 cm above ground level and then compress the soil around the roots.

The tomato seedlings should be spaced about 40 centimetres apart in the same row and about 1 metre between the rows.

Immediately after the transplanting work it is good to place a brace near the foot of each plant so that it can support the plant during its development. Excellent guardians are the bamboo canes. Alternatively, you can find rigid plastic braces. Personally, we use iron rods (those used for construction) cut to size and stuck in the ground with the help of a mallet. They are practically indestructible and reusable.

Now that both the plant and the brace have been placed on the ground, all that remains is to wet the soil around the stem abundantly to facilitate the rooting of the plants.

Tomatoes need a lot of water, especially during dry periods.

In normal periods, on the other hand, it is not advisable to over-water them because excess humidity is one of the main causes of apical rotting of the tomatoes and splitting of the fruit. Water a little and regulate.

Avoid wetting the fruit and foliage and pour water directly at the root of the stem.

As recommended in the previous article, the tomatoes need support because otherwise, due to the weight of the fruit, the plant would break on itself. If we have placed a suitable guardian near the root of the stem, as the plant develops it is good to tie it to the guardian making a very slow turn around the stem to allow it to swell further.

Absolutely avoid the use of iron wire, or cords too thin to tie the tomatoes to the brace because, with winds a little sustained, these could seriously damage the stem; there is the trade of rolls of rubberized and partially extensible wire that are ideal for tying tomatoes.

Watermelon

The fruit of the watermelon is usually very big, it can reach 25 kg, but for the family garden there are also varieties with smaller fruit, called "baby watermelons", more suitable for the consumption of an average family.

Ideal climate. The climatic conditions are the same of the melon, the watermelon is native to the warm climates, it has a seed which is born over the 24 degrees and then grows up well if the temperatures are around the 30 degrees, for this reason it is a typically summer vegetable and if the climate is a little rigid, we have to think to tunnels or mulching with black sheets in order to warm up the plants better. A temperature below 14 degrees can stop its growth, which can damage the harvest.

Soil. The soil for growing watermelon must be rich and not arid, tending to be acidic (ph above 5.5). It is a crop that requires water and nutrients. Like many plants, watermelon is afraid of water stagnation, which causes root rot, so it prepares the soil with deep spades and enriches it by fertilizing it with manure, compost or manure, watermelon loves a rich bottom fertilization. If you want the watermelon to be sweet, take particular care that there is a good presence of potassium in the soil if it is not enriched with fertilizer (you can also use ash).

How and when to sow the watermelon

When to sow and transplant. The watermelon sowing must take place in spring, if you sow it in a pot to be kept in a protected crop you can start in March, otherwise, especially if you sow in the open field, it is better to do it between April and May to avoid the risk of low temperatures or late frosts. Also transplanting in the garden should not be done before April.

Sixth planting. After having thoroughly dug deep and prepared a well refined seedbed, sow the watermelon in small posts, putting three or four seeds each at 3 cm depth. Leave two meters between one row and the other and no less than one meter between each plant along the row, watermelons are plants that take up a lot of space and ask a lot from the ground. After the seedlings have trimmed, it is essential to thin them out, leaving only two per post.

Cultivation and irrigation

Mulching. Watermelon benefits a lot from mulching. In addition to saving work when weeding weeds, mulching heats up the soil and prevents the fruit from resting on the ground, protecting it from rotting and pests.

Pruning. You can prune the watermelon plant by cutting off the apical bud to prevent it from developing in width and keep the energy of the plant to develop horizontally.

Weeding. If you do not mulch it is necessary to control the weeds and hoe the soil around the watermelon periodically to oxygenate it and keep it draining.

Irrigation. It is essential to provide water to the watermelons, frequent irrigation is needed during germination and transplanting, with the growth of the plant you need an increasing amount of water because the roots do not go particularly deep. Do not irrigate just before harvesting so as not to water the taste of the fruit too much.

Ripening of the fruit. We recommend turning the watermelons in the last stages of growth every 2 or 3 days, so that all sides can sunbathe. It is important to do this once on the left and once on the right, otherwise you twist the stalk and detach the fruit before harvest time. Another useful practice is to lift the fruit with a slat so that it does not rest directly on the ground.

Rotation and consociation. Let us avoid growing watermelons after other cucurbits and possibly also after solanaceae, all very demanding plants that impoverish the soil. Watermelon is good next to many plants, for example salads, spinach, onions, and tomatoes.

Plant diseases and pests

Watermelon can be affected by several diseases, the most dangerous are virosis, then there are some fungal diseases (the same that affect the melon).

As far as virosis is concerned, it is necessary to prevent it by paying attention to the tools used and keeping aphids under control.

In the fight against aphids, be careful not to use insecticides, especially in the morning when the flowers hatch: cucurbits have an entomophilous pollination, therefore pollinating insects such as bees and bumblebees are needed, which could become victims of insecticides, even those allowed in organic farming such as pyrethrum. Against aphids it is better to use natural remedies, such as nettle, garlic or soap and water. If you kill pollinating insects, you risk finding yourself without fruit.

Harvesting watermelons

It is not easy to know when to pick watermelons and knowing how to choose the right moment is fundamental to have a juicy and sugary fruit. A symptom that heralds the ripening is the skin that from wrinkled becomes smoother and "waxy", if you have seen a nice ripe watermelon you will understand what is meant, the shiny patina is scratched with the nail. Another symptom is the darkening of the tendril stands opposite the fruit, if it tends to dry the watermelon is ready to be picked. For those who have an ear, the watermelon can be beaten: if knocking makes a gloomy sound it is ready. Another hint of watermelon to harvest is a slight depression around the attack of the fruit on the plant.

The watermelon can be kept in the refrigerator for up to 20-25 days, in a domestic garden if you want you can make a scalar harvest in relation to consumption.

Variety of watermelons

Watermelon has been cultivated since ancient times, but today, varieties of American origin are preferred by horticulturists because they are smaller in size, we are talking about fruits weighing about 10 kg which are more suitable for the domestic garden, while Italian watermelons often exceed 20 kg.

The different varieties of watermelon, from the red or pale flesh up to the yellow, also the skin can be pale, dark, striated or not, there are also hybrids without seeds.

For a small domestic garden, we recommend the Sugar Baby variety, which is a very sweet watermelon with a small fruit, generally not exceeding 5 kg.

Zucchini

The soil and manure. Courgettes ideally require a soil pH of between six and seven, they are a very demanding plant in terms of organic matter and nutrients and for this reason they need excellent bottom fertilisation, take 1 kg of dry manure per square metre as an indicative reference, more than five times as much if it is mature manure. The courgette should therefore be planted in well fertile and preferably sunny soil.

The climate. The zucchini is a plant of tropical origin, for this reason it requires a temperate climate and fears frost, below 10 degrees it stops growing, loves temperatures around 15 at night and 25 during the day.

How and when to sow zucchini

In the seedbed. The courgettes can be sown in March in the seedbed in protected cultivation, just place one seed for each jar, one cm deep with the tip facing down. If the temperature is around 20 degrees, the seed germinates in 4 days if it is warmer even less. The seedling can remain in the pot until the formation of 3 real leaves, usually 15 or 20 days, then it must be transplanted. The last transplant can be done around August 20th, with seeds planted at the beginning of the month.

In open field. Sowing in the open field, on the other hand, begins from mid-April, when the temperature stabilizes above 10/15 degrees, if it gets colder the growth stops and the plants remain dwarf. For sowing in the open air, 2 or 3 seeds are sown in each position, 1.5 cm deep.

The implant sixth. Courgettes are sown at distances of at least 100 x 80 cm, being plants that are demanding both in terms of space and nutrients.

Shade the plants in summer. The zucchini with its large leaves is afraid of excessive sunshine, in summer it can be useful to shade small plants with cloths or nets, especially at noon and especially in the gardens of southern Italy where the sun beats strong.

Rotation. It is best to let the zucchini produce for two months; the total cycle will be 3 months since it takes one month to get to production. After the three months it is better to reseed it to avoid the attacks of powdery mildew.

You can also eat the plant. The stem of the zucchini is quite fragile, you must be careful not to break the branches, if the plant is damaged when young it can emit side branches, once grown instead if damaged it stops producing. The tops of the zucchini are edible, you may want to use them in soup, remember when you go to remove the plant for rotation. The buds are also a little known but very sought-after vegetable, especially in some areas of Lombardy. In case of hail that would ruin the leaves, remove the leaves that are too crumbled.

Anticipate the harvest (warm bed and covers). In order to anticipate the harvest of the zucchini, you can make a hole in which to bury fresh manure under the seedbed. To repair the seedlings in spring (March and April) you can use plastic hats or polythene tunnels.

Support. There are crawling varieties of zucchini, it is worth supporting the stem with 120 cm poles to tie it to have better exposure to the sun, air the plant and be more comfortable to harvest.

Mulching. Mulching is a useful technique in growing zucchini, firstly because it reduces the work of weeding and weed control, saving the horticulturist a lot of effort, secondly because it avoids the fruits to lean on the ground and when the soil is wet can save them from rotting. It can be mulched with either cloth or straw.

Irrigation. The zucchini is a plant that requires a lot of water, because it produces many fruits that we are going to pick and also because it has very large leaves that breathe, you have to wet it at least twice a week. It is better to irrigate early in the morning, under the foliage, therefore trying not to wet the leaves, using water at room temperature. After sowing or transplanting, obviously, there is a need of watering, as for all the small plants of the garden.

Fertilization during production. It is useful to return to fertilize the zucchini plant when it starts to produce, you can use macerated nettle or pelleted manure, the plant requires mainly nitrogen and potassium. This is done after the first flowers appear.

Pollination and zucchini flowers. In order to produce the fruit, courgette requires pollination of the flower and it is necessary to consider that there are male and female flowers. Pollination takes place in the morning, with good weather and temperatures not too low, if it rains the insects do not come out and you lose the day of pollination. If the courgette does not pollinate, it becomes dark and the fruit rots. Fruits must be eliminated immediately; with a lot of small fruits the production of the plant stops. When harvesting the flowers, which you will find more detailed advice later, you should consider pollination and leave the females and a few males. It is better not to pick the flowers in the morning to let the pollinating insects work.

Greenhouse cultivation. If you grow zucchini in greenhouses or if you use anti-hail or anti-aphid nets with thick mesh, you must be careful that bees and bumblebees can enter and exit freely, otherwise you risk that there is no pollination and therefore no harvest.

Rotation and consociation. The zucchini should be sown in rotation in the garden, both because it consumes a lot of nutrients and therefore it is better to leave time for the soil to recover, and because its diseases (such as powdery mildew) do not return from year to year. It is better to leave at least three years before planting zucchini on the same plot of the garden and to alternate them with plants of the legume family that can enrich the soil with nitrogen.

The harvesting of courgettes and flowers

The harvesting of the fruit. The zucchini is a fruit that is harvested unripe, without letting it swell too much. As it ripens the zucchini becomes bitter, while harvested small to medium size is a vegetable with a better taste. In addition, after having produced three or four large fruits the plant stops producing, while if you harvest the zucchini promptly it continues to make a daily fruit for two months. Each plant can easily make a zucchini of 150 grams per day, so in the family garden two or three well cultivated plants are enough to cover the consumption of the family. The zucchini is harvested by taking the fruit in your hand and twisting the petiole gently, if you use a knife you must be careful not to transmit any diseases of the plant. Always be careful not to break the leaves, the wounds transmit virosis. If you want to go deeper, you can read the article dedicated to the zucchini harvest.

The production of a zucchini plant begins one month after sowing and can continue until the first frost, as temperatures drop, the size of the fruit is reduced and the growth time increases (if a fruit develops in one day in July, you need two in September and even 3 or 4 in October).

The harvesting of zucchini flowers. Courgette flowers like pumpkin flowers are delicious, both fried in batter and in different sauces and risotto recipes. Male flowers can be distinguished from female flowers (the male flowers at the base of the petals have a trumpet-shaped corolla), while female flowers are shorter because they have a petiole with ovary. They are all edible to leave the female flowers so that they can produce the fruit and pick only the males. The zucchini flowers should not be harvested in the morning, after pollination has taken place, otherwise it can affect the production of fruit.

Zucchini varieties to cultivate

There are many varieties of zucchini, of different shapes, colours and flavours, the plants are also distinguished by being early.

Here are some excellent cultivars of zucchini, optimal for the family garden:

- Zucchini president. Classic zucchini with elongated shape, dark green skin, good production, strongly subject to powdery mildew.
- Tuscan round zucchini. Fleshy courgette, ideal to be cooked stuffed.
- Roman courgette. Excellent variety of medium size, elongated zucchini with streaks on the skin and very sweet flesh.
- Crookneck. Gooseneck" shaped courgettes with yellow flesh.
- Trumpet or Genoese courgette. Fruit with a long, narrow tubular shape with swelling at the end.

Kevin S. Stevenson
RAISED BED GARDENING FOR BEGINNERS

CHAPTER 8 - How to Defend Against Plant Parasites

The plants, in general, could be attacked by various adversities: due to the climate or parasites. Even if we give them a lot of care and attention, plants, trees, flowers, flowerbeds can develop problems with the leaves (yellowing), trunk drying, etc.

Often the adverse weather conditions are complicit with the parasites, giving rise to perfect climatic conditions that allow them to proliferate relentlessly. Some of these pests such as aphids and cochineals (very common in greenhouses), for example, proliferate in arid environments or indoors.

It is difficult to estimate the damage that pests can cause to plants, but they are certainly very serious from both an aesthetic and reproductive point of view. These insect invasions have sometimes led to the loss of crops.

Fighting pests means implementing strategies that can eliminate the problem at its root.

Pests, prevention, and treatment: Snails

Plant pests or pests are among the most annoying and difficult problems to solve in indoor cultivation, so it is advisable to prevent any infestation. In this paragraph we will talk about how to prevent and eliminate snails and snails.

Snails and snails occasionally attack outdoor cultivation and are very rare in indoor cultivation.

Snails and snails are found on leaves and flowers. These animals thrive in damp and dark environments. They are rarely seen during the day because they avoid direct sunlight and go out to feast at night.

Snails range in colour from grey to brown and grow to a length of about 5 cm. Their bodies are soft and fleshy, they appear shiny with a light burr that snails secrete to retain moisture and improve movement. They have two small antennae which are the "eyes".

The snails are snails with a shell. Their conformation is identical to that of snails unlike the calcium carbonate shell which protects most of the animal's body. When a snail is threatened, it can be completely retracted into its shell.

These animals feed on the leaves. Holes can be found in the leaves and/or edges of leaves or pierced flowers accompanied by a silvery, slimy trail. A single snail can attack several plants in one night.

Using micro-pellet products is an excellent solution to protect plants in indoor and outdoor gardens: just sprinkle an anti-Snails in the soil, around the stems of the plants or around the pots to protect the plants from any attack. These products are not dangerous for people and pets.

The best way to eliminate snails and snails is iron phosphate, also called "ferrine phosphate". Another great solution is to use micro-pellet snail baits to eliminate the infestation.

Green Caterpillar: Remedies to eliminate the green caterpillar

Discover natural remedies to eradicate all types of caterpillars that attack your plants: green caterpillars, bog wort, cabbage and phytophagous; here is how to eliminate them.

The green caterpillar is one of the most common pests, widespread and feared by every grower, because it is present in any type of cultivation. It is a pest typical of traditional crops and - to a much lesser extent - of indoor crops. It is generally green in colour, but it is not uncommon to find different colours, such as dark grey, brown, and orange. So, let us see how to deal with it, how to prevent it and how to eliminate the families of green and not green caterpillars that attack our plants.

The green caterpillar is very common in spring and summer and can be found mainly among the plants of outdoor crops, in traditional outdoor gardens, such as decorative plant bushes, and in vegetable gardens. They are much less common in indoor cultivations, those inside grow boxes and grow rooms, where the environment is generally more circumscribed, but above all controlled and clean precisely to avoid the arrival of parasites and dangerous external elements. In particular, green worms attack plants with very green leaves, such as basil, salad and rocket, tomato leaves, chilli, and cabbage, but - in reality - these pests often attack rose plants and geraniums. It is no coincidence that, given the spread of these types of plants, they are also commonly called basil caterpillars or rose caterpillars.

Some families of these caterpillars feed on the leaves of the plants, other species prefer the inner part, in the pith, and attack the stem of the plant, in correspondence with the softer and even more easily attackable parts. Generally, the green caterpillars tend to eat mainly at night, whilst during the day they prepare their den by digging deep holes close to the plants which they then attack.

Green caterpillars represent the initial stage of lepidopterans and butterflies. Their body is generally thin (but some have a thicker diameter) and are usually long and soft in texture. Their body is divided into three distinct parts, even at first glance: head, chest, and abdomen. The particularity of caterpillars is their ability to camouflage themselves thanks to the colour of their body; in fact, they have the same colouring as the leaves, an aspect that makes them very difficult to spot and, therefore, to fight.

Each family of caterpillars has different sizes and colours and therefore the types of leaves and plants attacked will also be different:

Agrotites: the adults of the agrotites are lepidopterans of grey or dark brown colour, have a wingspan of a few millimetres, are about 2-3 mm long and the colour is usually green, the most common shade, but can also be pink, grey, and black.

Cabbages: the adult specimens of the cabbages are dark coloured lepidopterans and have a wingspan of a few centimetres. The caterpillars in the family of new born cabbages are generally green, slightly mottled and can grow up to a length of 4 centimetres, when they become clearly visible on the plants.

Phytophagous: You can find different families of phytophagous that transform and become adult lepidoptera, which take on different colours and sizes. Also, in this case the caterpillars are generally green, but they can also have different shades, especially if they are grey or brown and their body can be up to four centimetres long.

As mentioned above, caterpillars attack the soft leaves and stems and feed on the softer part inside. The branches and leaves attacked by the caterpillar wither because they do not receive water and nutrients properly. If these caterpillars also attack the main stalk, the whole plant will begin a process of progressive deterioration that will lead to the death of the plant. If the green worm infests only one branch, it will die - instead - only that branch.

Remember that plants are also susceptible to infections and mould as a result.

Prevention

How to prevent the arrival and attack of caterpillars on plants? Surely, as mentioned above, starting a cultivation indoors - i.e. an indoor crop - almost eliminates the risk of caterpillars. If - on the contrary - you have decided to start a cultivation outside, the classic outdoor cultivation, keep the seedbed and the germination mini greenhouses as much as possible inside before transplanting abroad; this is to prevent caterpillars from attacking and destroying the plants at a time when they are still very young and weak. In order to avoid the infestation of green caterpillars - and other pests - it is important to constantly monitor the growing area and clean it from wild grasses and plant residues before planting the plants. Pure Cinnamon extract is an excellent product to prevent caterpillar infestation, regardless of the species it belongs to cabbage, agrotites and phytophages will be eliminated with the same types of products.

How to eliminate caterpillars?

Various methods can be used to definitively eliminate an infestation of caterpillars. If you only have a few plants, the easiest and most immediate method to control and eliminate caterpillars is to physically destroy them. If, on the other hand, the infestation is more extensive, and you have already detected damage to the plants (in this case the caterpillars will be at most 25 centimetres away from the damaged plant). The most effective method in such cases is undoubtedly to use an organic product containing a living bacterium: Bacillus Thuringiensis. These bacteria debilitate caterpillars - and other animals harmful to plants - but are harmless to humans and pets. When caterpillars ingest the bacteria, they stop feeding - often paralyzed - and die within a short time. When they die, however, the caterpillars release new generations of bacteria ready to attack other caterpillars. Remember that it is important to use the bacteria at the first sign of caterpillars.

Leaflet Miners

Plant pests or pests are among the most annoying and difficult problems to solve in indoor and outdoor cultivation, so it is advisable to prevent any infestation. In this paragraph we will talk about how to prevent and eliminate leaf miners, also called (mistakenly) leaf miners.

Foliar miners are not common in indoor gardens, the leaves outside are attacked occasionally, but it is still a pest, which must be kept under control to avoid infestations.

Foliar miners - or lepidoptera larvae - are usually found on the top of the leaves and inside the tissues.

Foliar miners are usually the larval form of various species of flies, lepidopterans, and cockroaches. These very small larvae are worms about 3 mm long, white, or green in colour. The adult forms are small flies about 2 mm long.

The appearance of the leaves is as if someone has carved scribbles on them. As they feed and dig the leaves, they lay their eggs deep down and continue to multiply. When they hatch, the larvae feed on the leaves until they are big enough to become pupae. The transformation takes place inside the leaf and once they emerge, they repeat the cycle tripling and form a large infestation. Foliar miners leave the leaves open to pathogens and fungi and - when they dig - in the leaves they create a reaction in the plant that emits sugary molasses that attracts ants and fruit flies.

Prevention

In outdoor cultivation it is possible to plant useful plants such as wild spinach at the edge of the garden to discourage pests. Among the products useful for the prevention of attacks from foliar miners are foliar sprays containing plant extracts and phenols or alternatively you can make a treatment (above and below the leaves) with Neem Oil.

Getting rid of leaf miners is a real undertaking. Putting natural enemies such as ladybugs into the cultivation area will help to fight the infestation. If some leaves have been affected and have the classic wavy embroidery on the top of the leaf, remove them from the plant. Nebulize capsaicin above and below the leaves, alternatively use a product recommended in these cases, according to the manufacturer's dosages to complete the operation.

The Cochineal and Coccoidea

The cochineals of plants - whose scientific name is coccoidea - are pests particularly feared by growers because they frequently attack all types of plants, especially those grown outdoors. In order to avoid being attacked by these pests, it is therefore important to prevent their arrival. Let's see, then, how to avoid their attack and how to deal with the situation when our plants are attacked.

The cochineals - which are very similar to aphids and belong to the great family of the Rhynchota - are generally quite dangerous, especially because they hide easily among the plants and it is, therefore, difficult to detect them, especially if you do not carry out a constant and frequent control on the branches and leaves. It is necessary to know that there are many types of cochineals and the most visible of the others is the family of the cotton cochineals, which can be more easily identified thanks to their white colour which stands out on the leaves.

Floury cochineals and coccoidea are very common in outdoor gardens, while it is rather difficult - at least in general - to find them in indoor cultivation. Cochineals attack a bit all types of plants, but they more commonly attack the fat and decorative ones, but also fruit trees and garden plants.

The mealybugs are usually present between the internodes of the branches, they fall into the knots. On the plants you can find small puffs of cotton, usually near the internodes. Coccoidea can be found on the lower page of leaves and stems. They can also be found at ground level, where the stem joins the roots.

It is important to know that cochineals tend to reproduce more vigorously in warm, moisture-free areas. Precisely for this reason, the summer periods are the most dangerous for the diffusion and the reproduction of these pests. To prevent them from arriving, it is important to water the plants properly and keep the growing environment clean.

There is a large variety of cochineals that differ in colour and body shape. Cochineals and coccoidea are closely related to each other but are named after their appearance. Mealybugs have this name because of their white floury wax covering their bodies. The adult females under the wax are about 2-4 mm long, have flat, oval, and segmented bodies. The males are like small white flies and the body is not covered by the wax layer. The cochineals are so called because the adult females produce shells resembling small humps on the stems and leaves of the plants.

These parasites attack the cracks on the surface of the leaves and - more generally - the innermost, hidden parts of the plants, which are poorly illuminated by sunlight. In particular, cochineals attack - in a particular way - environments with low humidity and little ventilation. As they spread over the plant, the cochineals start from a small colony and then progressively invade the whole structure of the plant, taking the sap from the leaves and gradually weakening the whole plant.

The females of the floury cochineals and of the coccoidea, in fact, nourish of the sap of the plants and it is they who represent the greatest danger for the plant, because they create grooves in the lymphatic channels, in order to nourish of the internal liquid. The males, on the contrary, have a very short life as they do not nourish and live only for fecundating the females.

When attacking the plant, these parasites produce the honeydew, that is, that sugary liquid which attracts both the fungi and the parasites. The action that results in a leech effect of the insects causes a weakening of the plant and the fall of honeydew causes soot infections on the stems and leaves. These pests carry various diseases that are harmful to plants.

If you notice the presence of ants, it is possible that there is an attack by cochineals, which - by producing sweet honeydew - attract sugar-loving ants.

Prevention

It is important to know that cochineals tend to reproduce more vigorously in warm, moisture-free areas. Precisely for this reason, the summer periods are the most dangerous for the spread and reproduction of these parasites. To prevent them from arriving, it is important to water the plants properly and keep the growing environment clean.

The first solution that can be adopted to buffer and contain the reproduction of scale insects is manual removal. It is advisable to wash the leaves attacked by the parasite with water and then expose them to direct sunlight, in order to create an environment hostile to the parasite.

Another of the most widely used natural remedies to fight in a natural way and eliminate cochineals - but also many other families of parasites - is white oil or - alternatively - tea oil, two liquids that are sprayed on the leaves of the attacked plants and create a thin repellent patina able to trap and kill the small invading enemies. It is a mechanical system, which does not affect the environment and people. The only drawback of this remedy is that it should not be used in summer, because the layer that forms on the leaves would prevent proper transpiration and death of the plant itself. On the other hand, it is also true that it is precisely the summer period that is the most subject and most sensitive to cochineal attack.

A remedy that is always useful to eliminate cochineal - in this and many other occasions when you want to fight parasites - is the use of antagonistic animals. In this specific case it is possible to use both ladybugs (which work with almost all types of insects that are dangerous for our plants) and wasps, which keep the coccoid away.

Another effective and recommended natural remedy to combat the aggression of all plant pests, including ladybugs - or coccoidea - is Marseille soap: just dissolve small flakes of natural soap in water (30 g of soap in a litre of water) and spray the liquid obtained in the evening hours, every 3 days, until the parasites disappear.

Traditional Remedies

If the natural remedies and cures to eliminate scale insects do not work, you can also use lemon-based products, which kill both floury scale insects and normal coccoidea on contact. There are also a number of traditional products, such as specific insecticides, which naturally work flawlessly and effectively remove and eliminate parasites. The only recommendation is to manage the doses correctly and read the instructions on the packaging of the individual products carefully, to avoid improper use of the insecticide.

Ants

Pests - i.e. small plant pests - are among the most annoying and difficult problems to solve in indoor and outdoor cultivation, so it is advisable to prevent any infestation. In this paragraph we will talk about how to prevent and eliminate ants.

Ants abound both indoors and outdoors. Most species that attack plants use them as "pasture" for aphids or vine bugs.

Ants nest in the soil or growing medium and travel through the trunk to the leaves to graze their flock of aphids and vine bugs.

Ants consist of 3 parts: the head, the thorax, and the abdomen. The legs are attached from the chest and the eyes, antennae, and mouth to the head. They usually reach a size of 2/5mm.

Ants form underground colonies and must dig holes to move around, which damages the roots of our plants. The aphids and vine bugs carried by ants are a threat to the plant as they suck the lifeblood. If they find a good situation to thrive, the ants create their nest inside the trunk of the plant.

Prevention

There are several methods to prevent ants from settling within the growing area:

- Water: ants do not swim, so building a water channel around the plants can prevent them from forming a colony.
- Some useful plants, such as cinnamon, cloves and bay leaves - if shredded - can be a powerful disincentive to colonize.
- Chemical Barriers: Boric Acid can create a barrier for plants, but sometimes ants also cross it, which get covered in dust and slowly die or bring the poison into the nest.
- Artemisia Absinthium: It transfers deterrent properties to the soil due to the presence and effectiveness of bitter principles with great respect for the biological balance.

To eliminate ants, you can use different natural products that act in different ways, with the common result of effectively eradicating them. The most used in gardens is Pyrethrum (or derivatives) which is a natural protector obtained from a plant of the chrysanthemum family. It is a lethal product for ants.

Thrips

Thrips are parasites - or pests - of plants and represent one of the most annoying and difficult problems to solve in indoor cultivation. Therefore, it is advisable to prevent possible infestations. In this paragraph we will talk about how to prevent and eliminate thrips with natural methods (biological control) or traditional insecticides (chemical control).

But first let us see what they are and how they behave.

Like many other types of parasites, they also attach themselves to the structure of the plant, to the leaves, and suck out the sap. These small insects represent one of the biggest problems of all growers, especially those involved in greenhouse and indoor cultivation, also because they reproduce up to 12 times a year and - once they reach adulthood - begin to fly and can, therefore, pass quickly from one plant to another.

Among the plants most attacked by thrips are hemp and cotton plants, but they also find other types and varieties of plants attractive. Their ideal climate - to spread and reproduce - is the warm one, so it will be advisable to watch over the plants especially in the summer season.

Thrips are not common unlike other pests, but - in certain greenhouse conditions - these animals can be very aggressive.

Thrips attack the leaves and are usually visible on top of the leaf. In winter, they hibernate and activate at temperatures above 16°C. In indoor cultivation, the artificial climate allows them to be active all year round. The eggs are first found under the leaves and then fall on the ground, and then hatch when temperatures are optimal (26°C to 28°C).

The thrips are about 1,5 mm long and are visible to the naked eye. The adult specimens develop wings but rarely use them, in fact they prefer to walk on the legs and fly only in case of danger. They have a dark colour ranging from yellow to brown. The larvae are half the size of adults, lighter in colour and without wings.

The thrips cut the leaves - through a structure that can be associated with a tool such as a saw - to pierce and scrape the leaves until they reach the sap on which they feed. On the surface of the leaves they leave irregular white or silvery patches, the leaf appears scarred and covered with white crusts. The thrips leave behind them black spots of excrement above and below the leaves. The damage caused by thrips initially resembles that of mites or leaf miners, but in more serious cases they cause the plant to lose its colour.

Thrips are parasites that attack numerous types of plants; among the most frequently damaged are tomato plants, vines, orchids, fruit trees, especially citrus and peach trees. The stings of these annoying animals suck the nutritive elements of the plants they attack and cause widespread depigmentation, which results in abnormal white spots on the leaves, thus causing a state of disease and suffering of the plant. This, in fact, facilitates the arrival and spread of infections due mainly to attacks of alternaria and botrytis, which mainly involve leaves and fruits.

Prevention

As for all the other types of parasites, also for thrips is the same advice as always, which we have seen in other posts of this blog dedicated to the fight against the most feared parasites: to avoid their spread we need to be careful often and avoid that they colonize our plants. To do so, it is advisable to keep the cultivation environment clean, especially when growing indoors, remove dead leaves and disinfect environments and equipment for daily use, to avoid the proliferation of pests and insects, but also mold and other dangerous organisms.

To prevent an infestation of thrips, it is possible to use yellow and blue chromotropic traps, very similar - in mechanism and functioning - to fly paper, which first attracts flies and then traps them. In outdoor gardens you can also use garlic to keep them away. Another recommendation is to increase protection, using natural products and Neem Oil which nourishes and defends the plants in a natural way.

To eliminate pests, it is possible to introduce natural enemies into the affected area, such as predatory mites. The most effective method to permanently eliminate thrips is to wash the plants with vegetable soap and then use a pyrethrum-based product.

If you prefer to use traditional chemicals (normal insecticides) to fight thrips and eliminate them from your plants, remember to always protect your eyes and hands, as these are potentially toxic substances.

Aphids or Plant Lice

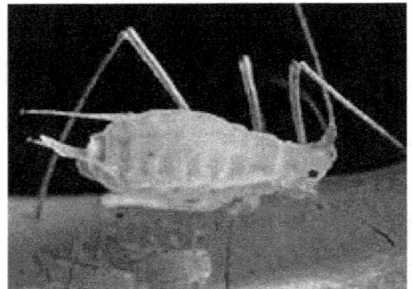

The aphids or lice that attack our plants are certainly one of the biggest concerns for indoor and outdoor growers. It is therefore of paramount importance to visually check and monitor all cultivated specimens frequently in order to detect the problem and prevent infestation; however, monitoring for preventive purposes is also extremely important.

In this paragraph we will talk about how to prevent and eliminate aphids, known as plant lice, both with traditional methods (chemical products) and with natural remedies and products, which can be easily made at home or - for those who want practicality - can also be purchased online or in specialized shops.

Among the many parasites that normally attack plants we find aphids, also called plant lice, or small insects - with a soft body and pear-shaped - of which we find hundreds of different species, which therefore have different characteristics, but all have in common the danger for our plants, especially ornamental plants (of all types) and all types of crops. That is why plant lice is a very common problem. The aphids are about 1 to 3 mm long, the body colour varies according to the specific family to which they belong and can range from yellow to green and brown to black, so it is not so trivial to recognise them immediately.

Some of these plant lice have wings and are covered by a layer of woolly wax, which they make themselves through the texture of their secretion.

The main problem with winged aphids is their great ability to turn from one plant to another and thus damage large plantations in a short time. The aphids that have lost their wings, on the other hand focus on reproduction and precisely for this reason are able to generate large colonies of dangerous lice in a short time.

One of the main characteristics of aphids - which allows them to be more easily recognized and distinguished from other parasites

- is the presence of a pair of horns present on the back of the abdomen.

Plant aphids - just like many other pests such as the whitefly - tend to colonize the stems and the lower part of the leaves; you can notice their presence thanks to their intense colour which often contrasts sharply with the green colour of the plant. Other families of aphids, on the other hand, tend to camouflage among the leaves and - in this case - it is more difficult to detect them and notice their presence.

But how do these insects behave? What exactly do they do to the plant?

The lice that attack the plants have a mouth equipped with an apparatus that is able to suck the sap from the plants and at the same time to release - in the very tissue of the plant - a particular saliva that induces the plant to form protuberances, which - in turn - protect the colonies of insects by providing them with food. This intense activity set in motion by lice on plants also leads to the production of honeydew, generated as a result of the waste of the sugary sap on which these insects feed, which involves the spread of sugar drops, which progressively invade the whole plant, favouring - consequently - also the formation of dangerous fungi and preventing the proper photosynthesis chlorophyll activity.

But that is not all, because honeydew also becomes appetizing food for other types of insects potentially dangerous for plants, such as bees and ants, which feed on sugar drops, further weakening the plant.

How they reproduce and what they cause

Plant lice prefer warm and mild climates, with temperatures ranging between 18 and 26 degrees centigrade, and opt for dry environments. In order to contain the proliferation of aphids, it is good to remember that these lice fear the rain, the wind and - more generally - the low temperatures; therefore it will be easier to find them in the warmest places and climates, in particular from spring to summer, and less in periods characterized by cold temperatures.

Aphids are insects as dangerous and harmful as they are resistant and able to reproduce. In particular, plant lice resort to the so-called "canning of the generations", a process which allows the female to keep inside her already formed daughters, which - in turn and even before being born - contain other insects in the embryonic phase. These - once given birth by their mothers - are already able to behave like normal adult aphids, so they will immediately attack the plant to feed themselves, weakening it even more.

Another strength of plant louse lies - as can be expected from their behaviour on plants - in their great ability to adapt to the environment, particularly when the climate is mild. Many families of aphids, in fact, often manage to resist even the action exerted by insecticides, both natural and traditional ones. However, luckily, there are many antagonistic insects that the aphids deeply fear, thanks to which it is possible to resort to them in order to contain the proliferation and then to progressively eradicate these insects.

The aphids feed on the juices of the plants by piercing the leaves and sucking the sap from the stalks, branches and leaves from the straw mouth. To obtain enough protein to thrive, the aphids suck in lots of sap, refine the protein and expel a sugar solution called "honeydew". This refined and concentrated compound attracts ants who ally themselves with the aphids protecting them from predators. The honeydew creates an ideal substrate for the growth of soot, which causes necrosis of parts of the leaf. Plants attacked by aphids have curled leaves, wilting of the plant and a delayed production of flowers and fruits. They carry viruses, bacteria and fungi and can quickly cause an epidemic.

Prevention

The most important months for prevention against plant lice are April and May, the spring period, when these dangerous insects are particularly strong and resistant.

In order to prevent the presence and spread of aphids, it is good to know that plant lice are transported by air for part of their life cycle, so - in the case of indoor crops for example - a thin filter in the inlet air intake helps to keep them away from your growing area. To make sure you create a hostile environment for them, clean thoroughly before you start indoor growing and check the stems and underside of the leaves periodically.

Always remember that most aphids cause the most damage when temperatures are warm (18-26°C) - i.e. when they find their ideal habitat for reproduction, as we have seen above - and they are very difficult to control because the very large, curly leaves protect them from insecticides or natural enemies.

One way to prevent the onset and spread of aphids is to constantly control your cultivation and your outdoor garden, especially at the edges against the wind, and to predict the presence of natural enemies, such as ladybugs and neuropterans, which effectively and naturally counteract the reproduction of plant lice.

Generally speaking, it can be said that constant control of cultivation and the presence of natural enemies and deterrents can counteract the reproduction and spread of the aphid population, which - in some cases - can be easily reduced without the need for treatment. In indoor cultivation - and for further prevention - a treatment with natural products (without pesticides) such as Agrobacteria's Protect Killer, K-Directin or a Biofortifying Spray is recommended.

How to eliminate aphids with natural remedies

Natural remedies against aphids can be implemented with great effectiveness especially at the beginning, when the problem is noticed or as a preventive treatment. Before treating aphids, it is important to check for the presence of ants, because it is much more difficult to control aphids when they are present, so - before any treatment can be carried out - they must first be eliminated.

The first step to take, as always, is to clean the leaves manually, in order to remove the insects, and cut off the parts of the plant already colonized. When the infestation of aphids is minimal, it is possible to spray the aphids away simply with cold water, this solution is particularly effective in outdoor crops. Secondly, if the infestation is still low, some natural remedies can be used.

For example, one of the most widely used systems against plant lice is nettle macerate (but also that of garlic, chilli or tobacco, which are natural repellents capable of annoying these insects), a technique that is also widely used in the world of organic farming, which offers its advantages, provided it is carried out several times. To facilitate and simplify the treatment, it is possible to use one of the nettle macerates commonly available on the market.

Another natural remedy - always in cases where the presence of aphids is rather low - is to use Marseille soap: just put small flakes of Marseille soap and water inside a sprayer, then shake and spray directly on the leaves. With this simple treatment, the aphids will tend to get annoyed and, therefore, move away from the plant.

Another natural remedy that can be used to counteract the spread of aphids in a natural way is Neem oil, a natural insecticide that also works effectively against recurrence.

In particular, inside the cultivations and indoor gardens, places where aphids have an easier life thanks to the artificial climate and the lack of natural predators - the situation is a bit more complicated, because nature comes little to our aid; even in these cases, however, it is possible to intervene in a very similar way to what we have already seen above, in the following ways:

1. introduce natural predators such as ladybugs into the cultivation area.

2. Aphids are very susceptible to fungal diseases when it is humid, entire colonies can be killed by these pathogens when the right conditions are created.
3. Spray a solution of water with garlic and cloves under the leaves.
4. Gently clean the plants with a vacuum cleaner and apply the vegetable soap to the lemongrass.
5. Use one of the traditional products against insects according to the methods indicated by the manufacturer.

If the infestation is already in an advanced state, it is advisable to use Pyrethrins-based insecticides. These products should only be used after dilution, preferably in the evening/at lights out, when the active ingredient is most effective.

Plant Mites

Plant pests or pests are among the most annoying and difficult problems to solve in indoor cultivation, so it is advisable to prevent any infestation. In this paragraph we will talk about how to prevent and eliminate mites (or red spider mites).

Mites, or red spiders, live more on the reverse side of the leaves, but also on the shoots. They can also be found moving on their web from plant to plant. Mites are most active in warmer climates.

Mites, or red spiders, are difficult to see with the naked eye as they are only 0.4mm long. They are arachnids (relatives of spiders) and have four pairs of legs, they have no antennae. However, unlike spiders, they have a unique segment of the body. Their colours vary from red brown to black, yellow, and green depending on the species. Mites are so tiny that most of these details can only be seen under a microscope.

Mites pierce the surface of the leaves, then suck the sap from them. These stings appear on the leaves as tiny brown dots surrounded by yellowed leaves. Identify the infestation by tiny dots on the leaves. You can see them as coloured dots on the underside of the leaves. When the mite population grows you can see silvery cobwebs using them as a bridge between branches and leaves. They carry diseases for plants.

Prevention

Most infestations begin when insects enter through the ventilation duct or another infested plant, or are introduced by the gardeners themselves, who are used as a means of transport for the garden. It is therefore a good procedure not to enter the growing room wearing clothes that have been outside recently, particularly in the countryside or garden. Using an insect and dust filter is a good solution to filter the air entering the growing area. Use Neem oil on plants as a preventive and nutritive element.

Mites thrive in hot and dry climates and multiply quickly (Mites hatching = 3:1 female: males, each female lays up to 200 eggs). The high humidity slows down the development and reproduction of the mites. This can be used in the vegetative growth and early flowering stages to slow population growth.

White fly

The aleurodidae - more commonly called whiteflies - are insects belonging to the Aleyrodoidea family, which - in turn - are part of the homopter, a very large species with over 1500 living subspecies. These white insects can destroy tender or leathery plants and transmit diseases.

They are not easy to manage, and different methods can be used to eradicate them over the course of a few weeks.

This white plant parasite has its origins in tropical countries, but - due to its nature, its great capacity to adapt to various environments and to resist even different temperatures compared to those of the places where it originates - it has managed over time to spread evenly throughout the world.

Certainly, given its origins, it is easier to find the white fly in warm, poorly ventilated, and humid places, such as greenhouses, where it causes the greatest inconvenience.

The most common aleurodids - which nest mainly on the stems and between the leaves of our plants - are the Trialeurodes Vaporiorum, better known as greenhouse aleurodids, precisely because they prefer to spread and shelter in damp and sheltered places, such as the small plastic tunnels that are installed in vegetable gardens, but also in real traditional greenhouses. Precisely for this reason it is commonly called aleurodide of greenhouses.

Originally from Central America, the whitefly has spread progressively even in the temperate and warm regions of our country (it is much more present in southern Italy and much less in northern regions). In the northern and central areas of our peninsula, in fact, it frequents almost exclusively greenhouses and - more generally - sheltered and covered cultivations; however - in some conditions - it is also possible to find them in open fields.

For this reason and - as we have seen - for its great ability to adapt to the surrounding environment, the plants that risk being infested by the aleurodide are many.

Whiteflies are insects that live in colonies and nest in the lower part of the plants, or on the lower part of the leaves. Once settled, they begin to feed on the sap obtained by sucking the ribs with their mouthparts.

The whitefly is very similar to the butterfly, which is why they are often also referred to as white plant butterflies or - more simply - white butterflies, because they are even pleasing in appearance. These parasites, in fact, could look like real moths, but they are relatives of aphids, much more feared and dangerous.

White flies have a body about 1.5-2 millimetres long, very soft and completely covered by a sort of waxy powder, which gives them protection and the typical creamy white colour.

The larvae of these parasites are small caterpillars and nest in the lower part of the leaves, nourishing - as we have seen - of their sap. Most species of insects belonging to the whitefly family reproduce best when the ambient temperature is 27-33°C.

How do aleurodids reproduce?

The aleurodidae reproduce rapidly and - precisely for this reason - it is particularly difficult to eradicate them; this rapidity, in fact, allows a massive proliferation: generations of insects reproduce consistently throughout the year.

The adults, usually, are found on the upper part of the leaf of the plant, flying as soon as the plant moves. The female specimens, on the contrary, lay their eggs in the lower part of the leaf and each female can lay about 100/150 eggs (in some cases it can even reach 200). About 12 days after the laying, the neanids will be born, which are ready at the age of majority. At this point these insects are to all intents and purposes whitefly able to attack the plants and all this happens within about a month.

The whiteflies reproduce sexually, but for some species there can also be parthenogenesis.

Some species of these white insects regenerate only once a year (this is the case for example of the species attacking the olive tree), but - as a rule - they can have 2 to 4 cycles each year. However, if the conditions of the environment are particularly favourable, the numbers can be much higher. Greenhouses, for example, are a perfect environment both to welcome them and to accelerate their reproduction.

Whiteflies - as mentioned above - are common pests found in gardens, both indoors and outdoors. Usually they hide behind the lower part of the leaves and feed there on their sap, causing yellowing and weakening the plant; in cases where the plant is attacked in a massive way, it begins to progressively defoliate and weaken until it dies.

The aleurodids - as we have seen - are insects that genetically feed by sucking and - in this way - can also spread viruses and bacteria, producing a lot of honeydew, and allowing the development of soot. These white plant pests are generally visible to the naked eye - although they are small - but if you have doubts and want to be sure, you can shake the plant. Once the branches and leaves are moved, you can see a mass of tiny white flies taking flight. In this way, you will have the certainty of their presence.

Which plants affect the aleurodide?

The aleurodidae - or whiteflies - are parasites that feed on many varieties of plants, in particular they attack begonia, dahlia, fuchsia, cyclamen, but they can also easily be found on many other types of plants, both garden and orchard, even on very young trees.

The whiteflies affect in particular - as we have seen above - all the plants cultivated in the greenhouses, but there are, however, some of them which are affected, in a way, more than others. Among these we find tomatoes (perhaps you might also be interested in the guide to growing tomatoes) grown very often in greenhouses, but also aubergines, watermelons and also many ornamental plants, among which - in a particular way - it is worth mentioning poinsettias.

But there is more, because there is a specific family of aleurodids that attacks citrus fruits in a way and - for this reason - identified with the name "citrus white fly".

During the winter period, the aleurodehyde frequently nests among the leaves of vegetables, particularly in the leaves of cabbage, where they feel more sheltered, and then move away with the arrival of mild and cold temperatures.

However, it is good to specify - for completeness and precision - that these white parasites, identified with the name "white fly" or "greenhouse fly", in reality, do not represent one only species; there are, in fact, several subfamilies of this insect which can infest with the same modalities and create very similar damages. For convenience, we identify them all with the more generic term of whitefly or aleurodidae.

In this regard, we point out that another very common insect of the aleurodide is the "aleurodida tabacii" or tobacco aleurodide.

Damage created by the whitefly

The damage caused by the whitefly, unfortunately, is comparable to that of aphids, with the difference that - in this case - the fight is much more complicated, also because it seems that they quickly become resistant to the various active ingredients.

The damage caused by these insects are:

- The stings: the whiteflies suck the sap from the plants, as a result of which there will be sap removal and reactions from the plant, necrosis and leaf drying. There will be loss of vitality, colour, and productivity.
- Honeydew: Plants release adhesive honeydew, and this can contribute to the formation of mould on the plants. In addition, this is an obstacle to chlorophyll photosynthesis, which is accompanied by the development of cryptogams and product damage. The leaves appear stained, reclined and lose vigour.
- Transmission of virosis: whiteflies are virus vectors, particularly on the tomato plant, where this weed is a frequent problem.

How to prevent and natural remedies to defend your plants

Various strategies can also be implemented to prevent and combat whitefly.

Buy plants only from serious, professional dealers, who you trust, who make a preventive fight.

Protect the plants during the transition from the nursery to the greenhouse/growing area by means of fine mesh nets, which can prevent even the smallest insects from passing through.

Also, the place where you grow must be well protected and isolated from the outside, with special screens.

Very important is the periodic monitoring of weeds, especially in areas close to the plants you want to protect.

Provide yellow chromotropic traps and place them about 10 cm away from the plants, so that whiteflies can remain trapped.

Furthermore, it is recommended to keep the temperature of the indoor garden or greenhouse below 27°C, in order to hinder the reproduction of the whitefly, which - as we have seen - fears the cold. It is also necessary to clean the plants with lemongrass vegetable soap. The use of a dust filter in the inlet air duct can prevent whitefly from entering.

Prevention

But what can you do when the white fly has already arrived in our garden or orchard?

Whiteflies are an important problem and a danger not to be underestimated, especially because they reproduce quickly, becoming numerous in a short time over an entire crop. However - and this is the good news - they are not impossible to eliminate. The important thing, however, is to act now so that the damage can be contained.

First of all, it should be remembered that the aleurodid - being equipped with wings just like butterflies - flies from one leaf to another and from one plant to another, so trying to remove these insects manually or detach part of the plant - for example, as is common for rose aphids - is hardly ever a sufficient method. It is effective for removing larvae, but it does not help to fight the already formed and winged insect.

In any case, as a first attempt, it is always worthwhile to implement these systems.

Secondly, yellow chromotropic traps can be used to catch and stop adult whitefly to fight the aleurodids. These are strips of glue coloured yellow, which first attract these annoying insects and then imprison them (in essence, they work just like the strips to kill the flies we usually use during the summer). The yellow chromotropic traps should be hung about 20 centimetres above the plant to be protected and - as seen above among the preventive systems - it is advisable to place them in the growing space or in the greenhouse before placing your plants.

Another way to prevent and hinder the proliferation of whiteflies in cultivation is to create an inhospitable environment for these pests who hate cold and love high and humid temperatures: ventilate the greenhouse (or growing environment) frequently, allowing cold air to enter and spread.

Another effective - and always natural - way to fight these white plant gnats is to spread natural enemies in the protected growing environment, thus triggering a biological fight.

Among the natural enemies of whiteflies, we find the curvy "encarsia", which lays its eggs right among the whitefly's enemies, immediately triggering a biological battle.

But the biological fight against the aleurodid can also be carried out using the chalcidoid hymenoptera, or the Encarsia tricolour, insects that manage to contain - quite effectively - the aleurodidae, especially if they do not use insecticides that slow down their development.

But that is not all, because - in specialized shops - you can also find bacteria that infest both eggs and adults of aleurodide: these are Beauveria bassiana and Verticillium lecanii.

Finally, another remedy always effective to protect the garden from external attacks is represented by ladybugs, which are antagonists not only of aleurodids, but also of many other dangerous parasites.

Defending against whiteflies is a difficult battle to fight. In fact, these parasites lay their eggs very quickly and this leads to continuous aggression against the plant. In addition, another characteristic of aleurodidae is their ability to resist normal, commonly sold pesticides and this is due to the layer of wax that covers the eggs and protects them from enemies, including insecticides.

The white butterflies, in fact, are particularly strong and resistant, so much so that they adapt quite easily to the various active ingredients of the products used; for this reason it is advisable to vary - from time to time - the type of product and the active ingredient, to prevent these parasites from getting used to them.

Organic remedies and traditional/chemical insecticides

Beating the whitefly with an organic and natural product is not so easy, also because - nesting in the lower part of the leaves - they often manage to escape treatment.

Among the natural remedies recommended to fight them is neem oil and pyrethrum, which can kill the aleurodide. Alternatively, it is advisable to use garlic or hot pepper macerate, which have a repellent effect against the parasite.

However, the action of chemical insecticides is the one that offers the best results now: it is recommended to carry out close treatments with ad hoc remedies, one every seven days for a period of about 30 days.

The most recommended products are those that include pyrethrum.

Pest Prevention in Indoor Farming

Pest attack is one of the most frequent causes of crop failure, both in soil and in hydroponic systems. Very often it is more difficult to manage nutritional deficiencies.

Prevention is the best way to deal with plant pest infestations.

What do we mean by prevention? We mean essentially cleaning up and restricting access to unwanted organisms, the basic rules are:

Avoid having debris and plant matter on the floor (soil, dust, leaves etc.).

Always keep your tools clean (scissors, containers, pHmeters and conductivity meters).

Avoid as much as possible that living organisms (insects, humans, etc.) have access to the grow box where you are growing. Install a filter that prevents the ventilation system from letting insects in with the air and control access and cracks.

It is a good rule to use clothes that you only wear when entering the grow room, the same for shoes. Pets are of course banned from the grow room.

Before putting a new plant into a grow box where there are other uninfected plants, leave it isolated for a few days and see if it shows signs of pests and diseases. Once it has passed the test it can be inserted together with the others.

Thanks to these measures you will be able to greatly reduce the risk of pests on your plants, but you can never be sure that they will not attack.

Possible infestations include:

- insects: which attack foliage and stems and rarely the roots (root aphids).

- Mushrooms: They can develop on both leaves and stems but become dangerous when they attack the roots.
- Nematodes: small vermiform organisms that attack the roots. Some varieties are beneficial.
- Mites: Tetranichids or "spiders" are among the most formidable in indoor crops.
- Viruses: this is the worst thing that can happen to your plants in the grow box. These microorganisms start by deforming the leaves and then the whole plants until they slowly kill them. Unfortunately, there is no cure and when a plant contracts a virus the crop is lost.

Kevin S. Stevenson
RAISED BED GARDENING FOR BEGINNERS

CONCLUSION

Thank you for coming all the way to the end of this book, we hope it was informative and able to provide you with all the tools you need to achieve your goals, whatever they may be.

Raised-bed gardening has emerged as a great way to achieve the cultivation of genuine, tasty plant products at home for good health. Yet, many people fail to get all the benefits of this wonderful process due to lack of knowledge of the process. This book has tried to bring all the important points to the fore so that you can get all the benefits of this growing system without having to deal with the negative effects.

All you must do is follow the information provided in the book and follow the directions.

You can also get all the benefits of the process by following the simple steps in the book.

I hope this book will really help you achieve your goals.

Kevin S. Stevenson
RAISED BED GARDENING FOR BEGINNERS

www.ingramcontent.com/pod-product-compliance
Lightning Source LLC
Chambersburg PA
CBHW070344120526
44590CB00014B/1046